COACHING AT THE SHARP END

THE ROLE OF LINE MANAGERS IN COACHING AT WORK

Valerie Anderson

Charlotte Rayner

Birgit Schyns

The Chartered Institute of Personnel and Development is the leading publisher of books and reports for personnel and training professionals, students, and all those concerned with the effective management and development of people at work.

For full details of all our titles, please contact the Publishing Department:

Tel: 020 8612 6204

Email: publish@cipd.co.uk

To view and purchase all CIPD titles:

www.cipd.co.uk

For details of CIPD research projects:

www.cipd.co.uk/research

COACHING AT THE SHARP END

THE ROLE OF LINE MANAGERS IN COACHING AT WORK

Valerie Anderson

Charlotte Rayner

Birgit Schyns

First published 2009

Cover and text design by Sutchinda Rangsi-Thompson

Typeset by Columns Design Ltd, Reading
Printed in Great Britain by Short Run Press, Exeter

British Library Cataloguing in Publication Data
A catalogue record for this book is available from the British Library

ISBN-978-1-84398-238-8

Chartered Institute of Personnel and Development

151 The Broadway, London SW19 1JQ

Tel: 020 8612 6200

Website: www.cipd.co.uk

Incorporated by Royal Charter. Registered charity no. 1079797.

CONTENTS

ACKNOWLEDGEMENTS

The members of the University of Portsmouth research team responsible for conducting the *Coaching at the Sharp End* project, on behalf of the CIPD, were:

- ❖ Dr Valerie Anderson
- ❖ Professor Charlotte Rayner
- ❖ Dr Birgit Schyns
- ❖ Simon Turner.

We would like to express our gratitude to all those who were prepared to share their time, experiences and ideas with us by participating in the CIPD Coaching at Work Conference discussion groups, organisational interviews or the online survey.

Thanks go to those individuals and organisations who arranged for the distribution of the online survey. The research would not have been possible without Sally Vanson from The Performance Solution or the participant line managers at: Bromley Mytime Leisure Trust, the Children's Society, the Institute of Leadership and Management, London Underground – Operations, Middlesex University, the Ministry of Justice, Napp Pharmacueticals Ltd, Red Funnel Group and VT Group plc.

Particular thanks go to those individuals and organisations who participated in the interview process: Child Benefit and Tax Credit Office, KPMG, Southern Railway and VT Group plc.

Final thanks, of course, go to John McGurk at the CIPD for commissioning the project and providing constructive critique, support and encouragement for our endeavours.

FOREWORD

When the CIPD commissioned this report, we did so on the basis of evidence from our recent annual *Learning, Training and Development* surveys, which have shown that line managers are increasingly responsible for the delivery of coaching in the workplace. This was also evident in our 2008 *Developing Coaching Capability in Organisations* Research into Practice report – as well as in the rich stream of research and evidence that the CIPD has brought to bear on the world of coaching. Having identified line management to an extent as the load-bearers of workplace coaching and mentoring, we were concerned to know exactly how coaching was contributing or otherwise to the effectiveness of line managers and to good people practice and performance. We commissioned the research team from Portsmouth University to research the attitudes and behaviours of line management in delivering coaching and mentoring. The team has delivered what we believe to be an insightful and even groundbreaking piece of work. They broke new ground for several reasons:

❖ They approached the project as investigators with a brief to find out exactly what the coaching role meant for line managers and their organisations. They were not championing coaching, although like the CIPD they see coaching and mentoring as crucial aspects of HR. The starting point of this project was 'what's going on?' To that extent we ensured that the terms coaching and mentoring were absent because we were looking at behaviours, processes and attitudes, unadorned by any attempt to influence or promote coaching activity.

❖ The methodology – their research approach used a rich mix of good case study material, in-depth interviews and rigorously statistically verifiable data based on a large survey of line managers in key organisations. This has allowed us to say something about the underlying behaviours, processes and attitudes that drive coaching by line management.

❖ They used their extensive engagement with practitioners, both through their involvement as leading CIPD course tutors and in their practical day-to-day research, to reach out and find out.

This practice-driven curiosity and ingenuity has resulted in a publication that we believe will have wide-ranging implications for practitioners at all levels:

❖ It identifies and pins down the sets of behaviours that make coaching an effective method of line management. So using advanced statistical techniques, they were able to identify two types of line management coaching behaviour operating at various levels. *Primary coaching characteristics* comprise: a development orientation; a performance orientation; effective feedback processes; and successful planning and goal-setting activities. *Mature coaching characteristics*, which are also associated with a participative style of management, include: using ideas from team members; powerful questioning; team-based problem-solving and shared decision-making.

❖ The team was able – through the rich description of case study material, the insight from the numerous individuals and case studies, and the survey evidence – to demonstrate the real value that coaching brings, in both good times and bad. The resilience-building role of coaching is something that emerged from the project, equipping line management with a key skill.

❖ They were able to build on our previous work on line managers in learning and development and reward (Hutchinson and Purcell 2007), and our research on developing coaching capability (Knights and Poppleton 2008) to look at coaching from the trenches rather than from the operational headquarters. Much coaching research has focused on coaches and HR professionals, so evidence about the coaching role of line managers will add to our understanding and help us to design better coaching programmes.

❖ While coaching skills may be part of a manager's development 'toolkit', it is unrealistic to expect the deep rapport, level of confidentiality and 'boundary maintenance' expected from formal coaching relationships. The 'line manager as coach' role is better understood as a style of management, integrated within a move from a 'command and control' approach to a more participative style of management. Since coaching is about awareness and responsibility, this can make quite an impact.

However, the report warns that line managers need to be listened to. Whatever the perceived benefits of coaching, line managers will not engage if they feel that it is either an imposition from above – which doesn't recognise the other challenges they face – or a visionary approach from learning and development. The report identifies real obstacles to manager involvement, which are challenges for HR and the business. Not surprisingly, time constraints are the most significant barrier; organisation culture can get in the way; a perceived lack of skills and a lack of confidence to deal with difficult people can inhibit a coaching style of management. Yet resolving all of these issues can provide a big payback for the organisation.

Coaching and mentoring need to be positioned as interventions for the business, not just for HR or learning and development. Both of these functions have roles in design and support, but if line managers are to engage then coaching needs to have the imprint of business strategy – as evidenced by the organisations we spoke to, such as Southern Railway, VT Group and the Child Benefit and Tax Credit Office. That way the payback from coaching will be realised. This report will also reward those who read it and build on its insights.

Dr John McGurk

CIPD Adviser, Learning, Training and Development

EXECUTIVE SUMMARY

Line managers have a crucial role to play in people management and development and the 'line manager as coach' role is increasingly being advocated as an important part of line managers' responsibilities. The CIPD *Coaching at the Sharp End* project represents the first systematic research in the UK to assess the implications of the devolution of coaching to line managers. It examines the issues from the perspective of line managers and develops a framework through which line managers and HR professionals can work together to foster a coaching style of management.

Opinion is divided about the extent to which line managers can fulfil all of the requirements of formal coaching. While coaching skills may be part of a manager's development 'toolkit', it may be inappropriate to expect the deep rapport, level of confidentiality and 'boundary maintenance' expected from 'formal' coaching relationships. The 'line manager as coach' role is better understood as a coaching style of management, integrated within a move from a 'command and control' approach to a more participative style of management.

Information from the *Coaching at the Sharp End* project enabled a two-stage model of coaching characteristics to be identified, which together make up a coaching style of management. *Primary coaching characteristics* comprise: a development orientation; a performance orientation; effective feedback processes; and successful planning and goal-setting activities. *Mature coaching characteristics*, which are also associated with a participative style of management, include: using ideas from team members; powerful questioning; team-based problem-solving and shared decision-making.

Line managers identify time constraints as the most significant barrier to achieving a coaching style of management. In addition, organisation culture, a perceived lack of skills and a lack of confidence to deal with difficult people can inhibit a coaching style of management.

Three factors were shown to affect a coaching style of management: manager self-confidence, manager–team relationships, and the development and support that is provided. The research indicates that senior managers are more likely to exhibit mature coaching characteristics. This may indicate the inhibiting effect of the operational challenges faced by those who are closer to 'the sharp end', which may limit the extent to which they can fulfil the expectations of a coaching style of management.

Personal factors such as a manager's age, gender, level of qualification and experience as a manager do not determine the extent to which a coaching style of management can be developed. Coaching as a management style is also just as appropriate for organisations facing the challenges of hostile economic conditions as it is for those enjoying business growth and development.

However, successful implementation of coaching at the sharp end requires HR professionals to work with their line management colleagues to diagnose the most effective way forward in implementing and embedding coaching so that it becomes part of 'business as normal'. If a coaching style of management is to be consistently achieved in organisations, it requires that coaching is seen by top managers as a business issue rather than a learning and development department initiative and that senior managers communicate their commitment to coaching and role-model coaching characteristics in a consistent way. In addition, consistent coaching at the sharp end requires:

- ❖ Clarity about coaching roles and expectations are clearly communicated.
- ❖ Consistent attention is given to the time and resource constraints facing all managers, particularly those closest to 'the sharp end'.
- ❖ Appropriate and relevant training and support is offered to enable managers to develop and maintain coaching characteristics as part of their 'management repertoire'.
- ❖ Effective teamworking and relationships between and within teams is fostered and encouraged.
- ❖ Managers are encouraged rather than inhibited from developing confidence in their coaching capability.

THE CONTEXT FOR COACHING AT THE SHARP END

CHAPTER SUMMARY

❖ **Line managers have a crucial role to play in people management and development and the 'line manager as coach' role is increasingly being advocated as an important part of line managers' responsibilities.**

❖ **Line managers have to cope with a range of different responsibilities and competing priorities. It is unlikely that all line managers will have the personal qualities, skills and attitudes needed to fulfil a coaching role. The pressures on line managers to achieve multiple and frequently changing objectives may also mean that they have insufficient time and attention for people development and coaching processes.**

❖ **Three sets of factors affect the extent to which the idea of the manager as coach is likely to become a reality: individual managers' perceptions of their role and priorities; organisational culture and systems relating to coaching; and the support and development that is available.**

❖ **The CIPD *Coaching at the Sharp End* project represents the first systematic research in the UK to assess the implications of the devolution of coaching to line managers. It examines the issues from the perspective of line managers and develops a framework through which line managers and HR professionals can work together to foster a coaching style of management.**

INTRODUCTION

This report focuses on line managers, specifically the 'line manager as coach'. The report is grounded in the practical challenges that managers face, particularly as the implications of the economic downturn begin to hit home in their organisations. This report is as relevant to line managers as it is to HR professionals because it is managers 'at the sharp end' who make a difference to the development of their staff and are increasingly expected to undertake some form of coaching for them.

The manager as coach is not a new idea but it has been increasingly emphasised during the last ten years (Ellinger 2005). This report examines the manager as coach idea. It focuses on the role of the line manager as coach, but not on executive coaching processes, externally provided coaching services or the development of the role of internal 'specialist' coaches in organisations.

LINE MANAGERS AND PEOPLE MANAGEMENT AND DEVELOPMENT

Line managers are crucial for people management and development, particularly in an increasingly hostile economic climate characterised by diminishing markets and increasing competition for resources where difficult employment decisions have to be made. CIPD research has highlighted the importance of line managers for translating organisational imperatives into practice and encouraging 'discretionary behaviour' from members of their teams (Hutchinson and Purcell 2003).

The job of the line manager becomes more difficult by the day. Line managers have a wide range of responsibilities to undertake. They have to ensure that tasks are achieved and are increasingly expected to fulfil new roles in relation to people management and development without relinquishing any existing responsibilities. Their work is characterised by 'messiness' and multiple priorities, a situation that can easily lead to work overload, insufficient time and role ambiguity. Line managers can make a crucial difference to people development but very little is known about how they achieve this in practice: the factors that inhibit it and those that facilitate it (Hutchinson and Purcell 2007).

THE BACKGROUND TO COACHING AT WORK

The popularity of coaching as a development approach has come about as organisations increasingly focus more on workplace learning than on traditional approaches to training. In this way instructor-led training activities designed to impart knowledge and initiate skills are increasingly being complemented or replaced by work-based processes (that include coaching) that allow learners to acquire and apply knowledge, skills and attitudes in a more self-directed way (CIPD 2005). Coaching has become a widely used tool that can enable individuals to enhance their performance as organisations seek to realise benefits, such as: improved communication processes; higher productivity; greater clarity about goals and objectives; effective knowledge-sharing processes; increased creativity; enhanced staff engagement and the development of an effective leadership style (Thomas 1995; Clutterbuck and Megginson 2005).

Coaching draws on a range of disparate traditions, the most prominent of which have included (Parsloe and Wray 2000): sports coaching; life/career counselling; personal effectiveness/ 'fulfilment' interventions; and participative management style theories and frameworks.

The rapid expansion of the use of coaching at work means that practice has outpaced theory, so that (Jackson 2005; Griffiths and Campbell 2008; Ives 2008):

❖ Definitions of coaching vary from practitioner to practitioner and from organisation to organisation. This can lead to misunderstanding and a lack of consistency.

❖ HR practitioners, specialist coaches, managers and employees in organisations may have very different understandings about the purpose of coaching and its appropriateness for different situations.

❖ Very little agreement has yet been possible about the most appropriate way to manage and deliver coaching in an organisational setting.

What organisations, individuals and managers expect coaching to deliver will vary from organisation to organisation. Four sets of stakeholders can be identified as having an interest in the coaching activities being considered here (Jarvis 2004):

❖ the individual (sometimes referred to as the 'coachee' or 'client')

❖ the coach

❖ the line manager

❖ the organisation.

Over the last 20 or so years an increasing number of specialists have offered their services as 'coach' to individuals and organisations, and a vast and often confusing array of approaches have been identified (D'Abate et al 2003). No organisation will develop the same approach to coaching but there are a range of people who may be involved, including:

❖ specialist executive coaches (usually external to the organisation)

❖ internal coaches whose role in the organisation involves some coaching in addition to their other duties

❖ internal coaches whose full-time role involves coaching, either as a 'generalist coach' or in a particular specialist task area

❖ managers and team leaders acting as a coach to their team members through what can be called a coaching style of management (Rock and Donde 2008).

THE MANAGER AS COACH

The idea of managers as coaches is not new. Indeed, line managers coaching those who report to them may well be the main provider of coaching in over one-third of UK organisations (CIPD 2008b).

Linked with this many organisations aspire to achieve a coaching culture where a coaching style of management is adopted throughout the organisation and is embedded in meetings, reviews, one-to-one working relationships and team and workgroup processes (Megginson and Clutterbuck 2006).

While there is a vast and growing body of knowledge and expertise to support those in specialised coaching roles, very little attention has been paid to the implications for managers of the development of a coaching culture or for managers whose day-to-day role now involves them in coaching their team members. This report represents the first systematic assessment of these issues in the UK.

THE RESEARCH PROJECT

Given the lack of attention so far paid to the issues surrounding the line manager as coach, this research project set out to assess the implications of the devolution of coaching to line managers and to provide practical guidance appropriate for line managers to enhance their effectiveness in their role as coach.

The specific project objectives were:

❖ to investigate the implications of the development of a coaching culture for the role of line managers

❖ to examine the extent to which line managers report using behaviours associated with a coaching style of management

❖ to assess the individual and organisational influences on a coaching style of management

❖ to develop a framework through which HR professionals can work with line management colleagues to foster managers as coaches.

The research made use of three main approaches to gathering data. First, data from discussion groups involving 95 participants representing 69 organisations at the CIPD Coaching at Work Conference in November 2008 provided useful information about the challenges and opportunities of developing a coaching culture in organisations. In addition, in-depth interviews with four organisations provided the opportunity to probe into issues surrounding the reasons for the introduction of coaching in their organisations and the implications for the role and expectations of line managers. These discussion groups and interviews were held mainly with HR professionals and coaching specialists.

The third important part of the research was an extensive online survey for line managers to find out about coaching at the 'sharp end'. Survey respondents came from a wide range of organisational types and sizes and represented different levels of seniority, age, gender and backgrounds. Over 500 managers from ten organisations were enrolled to the survey and their contributions are gratefully acknowledged (see Appendix 1). A copy of the survey questions is included in Appendix 2.

REPORT STRUCTURE

Chapter 2 draws particularly on the insights of HR and coaching specialists who participated in the 'sharp end' interviews and discussion groups. It considers the implications of the development of a coaching culture for the work, practice and people development behaviours of line managers. Specifically it considers whether the line manager as coach is a realistic and feasible aspiration given the range of responsibilities and priorities (such as performance management, maintenance of operational processes and employee reward) that managers have.

Chapter 3 presents a two-stage model of a coaching style of management based on the outputs from the *Managing at the Sharp End* survey and uses information from it to highlight the behaviours and characteristics that comprise a coaching style of management as well as the barriers that inhibit its achievement.

Chapter 4 provides further in-depth examination of the factors that influence a coaching style of management: both inhibiting and facilitating factors. It proposes a model of coaching at the sharp end that organisations can use to direct their effort if they wish to introduce and embed a coaching style of management in their organisations.

Chapter 5 draws together the features of the research, both qualitative and quantitative, to develop a model that HR professionals can use with line management colleagues to foster a coaching style of management at the organisational and individual levels.

A COACHING CULTURE: IMPLICATIONS FOR LINE MANAGERS   **2**

CHAPTER SUMMARY

* A coaching culture – where a coaching style of management is adopted throughout the organisation – is increasingly advocated as a means to meet organisational and individual development goals leading to: improved performance; enhanced confidence; effective integration of organisational learning and development processes; robust talent and career management; and better relationships with customers and other external stakeholders.

* Establishing and embedding a coaching culture is not for the faint-hearted; it takes time and there are obstacles to overcome. Specifically, organisations must face up to the challenges of: an 'inhospitable' organisation culture; lack of clarity about coaching styles and expectations; and time and resource constraints.

* There is no 'one right way' for the development of a coaching culture. Options include: a centralised and structured approach; an organic and emergent process; or a 'tailored middle ground' route.

* Opinion is divided about the extent to which line managers can fulfil all the requirements of formal coaching. While coaching skills may be part of a manager's development 'toolkit', it may be inappropriate to expect the deep rapport, level of confidentiality and 'boundary maintenance' expected from 'formal' coaching relationships.

* The line manager as coach role is better conceived in management style terms as a coaching style of management, integrated within a move from a 'command and control' to a more participative style of management.

INTRODUCTION

This chapter explores what is meant by a coaching culture and examines the implications for line managers operating 'at the sharp end'. A coaching culture has been defined as an approach where 'coaching is the predominant style of managing and working together, and where a commitment to grow the organisation is embedded in a parallel commitment to grow the people in the organisation' (Clutterbuck and Megginson 2005, p19). The idea of a coaching culture can be an appealing proposition promising a win–win situation where both organisational and individual development goals can be met. Although tension between individual and organisational goals may lie 'beneath the surface' (Knights and Poppleton 2008), a situation where 'people coach each other all of the time as a natural part of meetings, reviews and one-to-one discussions and team activities' is attractive (Hawkins and Smith 2006, p105).

This chapter draws on information from facilitated discussion groups and semi-structured interviews involving over 90 people from more than 70 organisations. The experiences of those whose organisations have gone some way in the development of a coaching culture provide the basis for an examination of what led them to this journey as well as the obstacles and challenges they faced and the implications for the role of the line manager.

ROUTES TOWARDS A COACHING CULTURE

The journey towards a coaching culture has been characterised as a staged process (Clutterbuck and Megginson 2005):

* **nascent** – coaching is seen as a specialist activity separate from 'normal' management processes

* **tactical** – individuals are coached as part of organisational performance management activities

* **strategic** – coaching is an 'expectation' of employees at all stages of their careers in the organisation

❖ **embedded** – coaching is used in all settings and levels throughout the organisation.

No two organisations will take the same pathway between these stages and, whatever route is taken, it will take time and involve a degree of experimentation with different behaviours (Whitmore 2002). Organisations will have to work hard to embed any coaching initiative and develop momentum and critical mass, at some point reaching a 'tipping point' where coaching is no longer seen as an initiative but becomes part of 'the way we do things around here' (Knights and Poppleton 2008).

A number of factors are likely to affect progress towards a coaching culture (Rock and Donde 2008; Clutterbuck and Megginson 2005; Hawkins and Smith 2006; Knights and Poppleton 2008):

❖ the extent to which there is a clear vision/purpose for coaching linked to business priorities

❖ whether buy-in is achieved from everyone as potential 'coachees'

❖ the scope and effectiveness of an appropriate learning and development climate to develop and sustain coaching behaviours and skills

❖ the provision of supporting 'coaching experts' or champions within the organisation

❖ the development of coaching measures and reward and recognition processes for coaching behaviours

❖ whether the development of coaching is managed and embedded throughout the organisation over the long term.

A review of what has been written about a coaching culture suggests that this journey is not for the faint-hearted; it takes time and there are a number of potential obstacles in the way. Nonetheless, its benefits can include significant performance enhancement, transformational culture change and important improvements to management and leadership capability and style (Hawkins and Smith 2006).

CIPD studies have been able to track the drivers and context that have promoted a coaching culture over a number of years. In 2004 (CIPD 2004) the focus was on perceived benefits for individual performance. Four years later (CIPD 2008a), a broader range of organisation-wide issues formed the context for coaching (see Table 1). The evidence suggests, therefore, that in addition to the demand for individual performance, HR professionals and others are articulating organisation-wide reasons to develop a coaching culture.

Table 1: The context for coaching	
CIPD research in 2004 (Jarvis 2004)	CIPD research in 2008(CIPD 2008a)
❖ improving individual performance ❖ dealing with underperformance ❖ improving productivity ❖ career planning/growing future senior staff	❖ general personal development ❖ wider management/ leadership development ❖ performance improvement ❖ achieving behaviour change ❖ support during transition ❖ management capability-building ❖ development of senior executives ❖ organisational culture change ❖ specific organisational objectives

A clear priority for the *Coaching at the Sharp End* project was to probe more deeply into these aspirations and to assess the drivers and the obstacles as they are experienced by organisations that have embarked on a journey towards a coaching culture. HR and coaching practitioners contributed their views as part of a facilitated discussion process at the CIPD Coaching at Work Conference in November 2008. In-depth interviews with organisations that have gone some way towards achieving a coaching culture enabled a further probing of the issues. An overview of the questions that they tackled can be found in Table 2.

Table 2: Discussion and interview questions	
Coaching at Work Conference discussion questions	**Coaching at the Sharp End interview questions**
❖ Why bother with coaching? What does a 'coaching culture' have to offer managers and employees in your organisation(s)? ❖ What are the obstacles to coaching in your organisation(s)? ❖ Can a line manager also be a coach? What factors encourage this and what factors make it difficult or impossible? ❖ Is HR still committed to coaching in the organisation(s) where you work? ❖ If yes – why? ❖ If no – why?	**Background and context questions** ❖ Why did your organisation introduce coaching? ❖ What does the term 'coaching' mean around here? ❖ From your perspective, what does coaching promise? ❖ In your experience, what are the obstacles to coaching? ❖ How does the approach you take to coaching affect line managers? **The manager as coach questions** ❖ How would you describe the idea of 'the line manager as coach'? ❖ In practice, what does this mean? ❖ Thinking about 'the line manager as coach', what do managers here do well and what could they do better? **Support for managers' development questions** ❖ What support arrangements are available to help line managers develop relevant coaching skills? ❖ What other means of support would be helpful? **Final question** ❖ In your view – what is the future for coaching?

WHY BOTHER WITH A COACHING CULTURE?

In addition to the motivations for coaching identified in previous studies, this study identified some new reasons for coaching, including the opportunity for coaching to form part of effective talent and career management processes, and the prospect of fostering effective coaching relationships with customers and other external stakeholders. Table 3 provides examples of some of the challenges that coaching has been used to address.

Table 3: Why bother with a coaching culture?	
Culture change	'[Coaching was part of] quite a deep analysis of what we thought we really needed to do to embark upon a change journey.' (Andy Farrar, CBO/TCO)
Leadership development	'[We] introduced a leadership programme for about 250 of our middle and senior manager population. It was a huge investment in terms of money, time, resource . . . We launched into this year-and-a-half long leadership programme that really looked at equipping managers with the core skills to do their job. Many of them had been promoted through technical ability – particularly in the railway industry that's quite common – as opposed to their people skills. So it was really to try and give these managers a toolkit . . . of how to manage and how to give them the people skills and confidence to deal with people.' (Zoey Hudson, Southern Railway)
Talent management	'We want the managers to look at their teams in terms of talents, and in order to do that and to grow them you need to have that coaching mindset going all the time – the message [is] not to see [coaching and talent] as two HR initiatives. These [are] two business initiatives that sit alongside each other . . . intertwined.' (Michael Staunton, VT Group plc)
Customer relationships	'Coaching tools . . . [are] used by front-line staff to: question the customers and to recognise the style that the customer may want to be talked to in, [and] to help them ask the right questions, get the information quickly [so] they can get to the root cause of the problem [thereby] . . . giving a much better customer service.' (Andy Farrar, Child Benefit and Tax Credit Office)
Performance reasons	'Because we're a service organisation our people are the most important part of the business and we've got a very strong focus on enabling our people to be the best they can be. We have a series of initiatives to support that and coaching plays a very big part. We put a very strong emphasis on creating the capability within the organisation for people to have coaching conversations, as well as the discreet, off-line one-to-one coaching. So it's very much viewed as forming both part of the overall talent agenda and also incorporating much bigger parts of the firm's broader people agenda.' (Sara Hope, KPMG)
Management style	'[Managers now are] facilitating their meetings in a coaching style as opposed to feeling that they have to come with all the agenda laid out and all the answers for their people . . . which sounds really simplistic but in the rail industry that was the culture, that was the kind of command and control culture; you were a manager and you had to have the answer to everything . . . so that is quite a shift in culture for this industry.' (Zoey Hudson, Southern Railway)
Integrating learning and development processes	'A person may choose to see a coach if they're part of the leadership track . . . or they've got feedback from a development centre . . . they might find it useful to go and see a coach to help them create a development plan.' (Sara Hope, KPMG)

Information from the discussion groups and interviews also allowed for a deeper probing into the importance of a coaching culture as part of wider culture change processes. Three interrelated factors were highlighted within the overall culture change 'agenda' (see Figure 1):

❖ the objective of developing a people-centred culture

❖ the prospect of fostering more effective relationships within the work environment

❖ the chance to develop management style in organisations away from a 'command and control' towards a more participative approach.

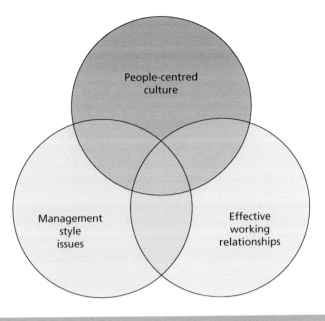

Figure 1 ❖ **Culture change issues**

OBSTACLES TO A COACHING CULTURE

A coaching culture is an attractive proposition for a variety of reasons. However, there may be a tendency for those who have invested in a journey towards it to overstate its benefits and to overlook the obstacles that exist (Clutterbuck and Megginson 2005). Individual factors, such as a lack of self-belief or lack of clarity about performance weaknesses or learning needs may well inhibit the development of a coaching culture (Hawkins and Smith 2006). In addition, there are likely to be a range of other organisational factors that must also be taken into account. So discussion group participants and interviewees were asked to reflect on the obstacles that they had experienced.

Three important obstacles were identified through the discussion groups and interviews:

❖ organisational culture

❖ lack of clarity about coaching styles and expectations

❖ time and resource constraints.

Concerns about an 'inhospitable' corporate culture and the challenges of time and resource constraints where coaching is concerned are well documented in the coaching literature (Hawkins and Smith 2006; BlessingWhite 2008; Knights and Poppleton 2008). The *Coaching at the Sharp End* project also highlighted the importance – if a coaching culture is to be achieved – of achieving clarity throughout the organisation about what can, and what cannot, be expected from the process.

Participants highlighted different experiences with coaching, particularly the problems that can result when there is:

❖ confusion about whether coaching is 'remedial' or 'developmental'

❖ a prevalence of 'coaching sceptics' in some parts of the organisation

❖ conflict between coaching and other performance management and performance improvement processes.

The *Coaching at the Sharp End* interviews suggest that the approach taken to the management of the coaching process makes a significant difference (see Figure 2). Previous CIPD research (Knights and Poppleton 2008) has described three broad options for the management of coaching:

❖ **centralised and structured** – coaching is introduced with a high level of senior support and consistency and structures are used to initiate the process

❖ **organic and emergent** – variation in coaching practices is accepted and uniformity of approach is not seen as a key issue in different parts of the organisation

❖ **tailored middle ground** – some combination of a centralised and 'organic' approach is adopted.

Participating organisations in the *Coaching at the Sharp End* project represented all of these positions. It became clear that organisations with a centralised and structured approach had more clarity about the purpose of coaching than organisations that were more organic and emergent in their route towards a coaching culture. Although the organic approach is attractive where an organisation comprises a number of different businesses, styles and locations, a challenge to be met is the likelihood of different (sometimes competing) interpretations about the purpose of coaching and the expectations of the role of individuals, coaches and line managers.

Participants in the *Coaching at the Sharp End* project also reflected on the challenges of time and resource constraints and the close links with the attitude of line managers towards coaching. All of the organisations in the study who had gone some way towards a coaching culture reported the importance of 'selling' a coaching approach to their line managers (see Table 3 on page 8) through effective training and communication. All of the interview organisations had invested heavily up front in training managers in the tools, techniques

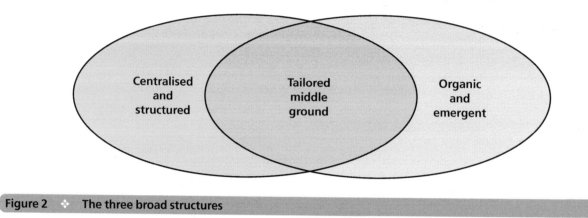

Figure 2 ✧ **The three broad structures**

and mind-set of coaching. This, in itself, can be a complex logistical exercise. In the Child Benefit and Tax Credit Office, for example, coaching training was rolled out to 5,000 administrative staff in seven months. Previously management training in coaching had been provided for over 500 managers in six months, something that was seen as an essential part of a wider culture change process.

CASE STUDY: ACHIEVING CHANGE THROUGH COACHING AS A STYLE OF MANAGEMENT – THE CHILD BENEFIT AND TAX CREDIT OFFICE

The background

Bad publicity, poor customer satisfaction and a demoralised workforce were just some of the daunting challenges facing the Tax Credit Office when it merged with the rather less controversial Child Benefit Office in 2003. Part of HR Revenue & Customs, the newly merged CBO/TCO is a large and labour-intensive operation employing over 5,000 people in the north of England. At the time of the merger it was characterised by a 'command and control' culture and over the following months and years a clear need for radical improvements to management capability, employee engagement and a customer focus was identified. In autumn 2006 Richard Summersgill, the director of the organisation, and Andy Farrar, his deputy, set about initiating a coaching programme as part of a wider business transformation process.

Coaching as a style of management

Since its inception in 2006 the approach to coaching at CBO/TCO has been to 'mainstream' it. Andy set about driving forward an approach 'led by operational people for operational people'. Four main principles underpinned the programme:

✧ Trust and invest in your own people.

✧ Take a practical approach rooted in workplace realities.

✧ Make coaching adaptable to different levels and functions within the organisation.

✧ Keep up the rate of momentum, including the rate of manager and staff involvement.

The vision was to achieve a situation where coaching was seen as 'business as usual' rather than being a specialised process remote from the everyday experience of everyone in the organisation. They wanted to embed a simple, practical coaching system relevant to every level in the organisation and based on operational realities and everyday conversational skills.

The first phase of this ambitious project was to initiate coaching as a style of management among all 1,000 managers in the organisation. Volunteers who were interested in delivering the first phase were invited to come forward. Eighteen people were selected to become licensed coaches. Once licensed, their role was to introduce coaching as a management style to their management colleagues through a series of two-day workshops and to offer support to managers in their use of this new approach in their everyday workplaces.

Two years on, managers exhibit visibly higher levels of confidence; they know much better what they are (and are not yet) achieving and what they need to do to improve further. Whereas managers had previously spent most of their time in isolated offices, the development of coaching as a style of management has given them the confidence to ask people for their opinions, unearth and exploit talent in their teams and drive things forward in the organisation that previously they would never have been trusted to do.

Coaching and front-line staff

Introducing coaching as a style of management to 1,000 managers in a context where command and control was so firmly embedded was challenging enough, but after six months Andy chose to 'up the pace' and take the coaching approach to all 5,000 administrative and front-line staff in the organisation. This time they advertised within the organisation and recruited 36 people who were licensed to deliver shorter (four-hour) 'coaching for confidence' events on a peer-to-peer basis across the organisation. Nearly 700 events were organised over a period of 12 months. The focus here was on equipping front-line staff to have the confidence to engage in coaching conversations with customers, many of whom find the Tax Credit system confusing and unhelpful and who are not always able to articulate their problems. This has enabled TCO staff to use their influencing and 'helping conversation' skills to coach customers to provide relevant information so that the TCO can get things 'right first time'. The coaching approach has also led to much greater engagement by front-line staff and the realisation that every individual in the organisation can make a difference.

Organisational outcomes

At CBO/TCO the introduction of coaching formed part of a wider transformational change process within the HMRC's 'Pace-Setter' programme. This focused on 'lean' working, quality and productivity improvements, and 'upskilling' of all employees. Continuous investment to embed and sustain coaching throughout the organisation has also been required. Subsequent workshops have enabled managers to have greater confidence in areas like giving and receiving feedback. It has not all been plain sailing. Andy Farrar is aware that not all managers have bought in to the new approach with equal enthusiasm and time, primarily the pressures of short deadlines and a relentless concern with productivity remain a challenge to coaching as a style of management. The time issue is a conundrum; on the one hand managers find it hard to allocate sufficient time to their 'coaching behaviours', but on the other hand Andy is aware that investment in time for coaching will release time in the long term for the proactive management of the business and so reduce the time needed to deal with reactive and operational problems.

A productivity increase of 25%, an increase in customer satisfaction of 6% (not withstanding poor publicity over the loss of Child Benefit data in 2007) and an increase in staff satisfaction of 11% speak for themselves. In 2005 CBO/TCO lagged behind the rest of HM Revenue & Customs in these indicators; by 2009 it was seven percentage points above the HMRC average.

POTENTIAL BARRIERS TO LINE MANAGER AS COACH

Internal stakeholders – top managers, HR practitioners, individuals, coaches and line managers – are all important if a coaching culture is to be achieved. Line managers are crucial if coaching is to become 'the predominant style of managing and working together' (Clutterbuck and Megginson 2005). Previous CIPD survey research (CIPD 2008b) suggests that almost three-quarters of organisations that report making use of coaching rely on line managers to have some involvement or to take the 'main responsibility' for coaching those who report to them.

However, little is known about the processes involved when the line manager is also the coach and opinion is divided about the extent to which the line manager can act as a coach. Alexander and Renshaw (2005) and Mayo (2008) argue that every manager should be concerned with the development of their staff and so coaching forms a natural part of the manager's 'toolkit'. On the other hand, there are a number of difficulties with the idea of the line manager as coach (Howe 2008).

First, coaching involves establishing a 'deep rapport', something that is not always possible for managers where the composition of their team may frequently change. Second, coaching involves an investment of time and is not always possible for managers facing various deadlines and work priorities. A third issue is that of 'mixed motives'. As managers have to deal with a range of issues, such as performance improvement, maintenance of operational processes, employee development and reward, so the addition of coaching as yet another role expectation is a further (possibly unwelcome) burden. While the idea of a coaching culture relies on a coaching style of management throughout an organisation, therefore, 'boundary issues' between line management and coaching processes may make it impossible to deliver a coherent, aligned coaching strategy.

Participants in the *Coaching at the Sharp End* project articulated four areas of ambiguity in the 'line manager as coach' idea:

- ❖ *The nature of the relationship between manager and subordinate* – to what extent can this be the same as the relationship between a coach and 'coachee'?

- ❖ *Conflicting priorities* – to what extent can ethical issues about a 'confidential coaching relationship' be aligned with a manager's responsibility for performance management and reward?

❖ *Skills and personal qualities* – to what extent are all managers able to demonstrate the skills, confidence and personal qualities that would enable them to demonstrate effective coaching behaviours?

❖ *Management style* – to what extent is a coaching style of management always appropriate in different organisational situations and contexts?

When discussing these issues, the participants highlighted that the expectations of a coaching style of management are distinct from the expectations of a coaching relationship at a more intense level, such as in executive coaching. They also indicated that the 'line manager as coach' role is better conceived in management style terms as a coaching style of management. It involves a move away from a 'command and control' and towards a more participative management style.

No clear consensus on this issue emerged; some participants argued that development is 'of itself' the function of management and so coaching sits squarely within this responsibility. Others suggested that the idea of a manager acting as a specialist coach with members of their team is problematic. Instead, they advocated a more general coaching style of management as a means of providing a reasonable 'coaching coverage' across the organisation.

This is an important issue, so participants were encouraged to describe the characteristics that comprise a coaching style of management and the following views emerged (see Figure 3):

❖ engagement with 'coaching conversations' (not a direct 'copy' of a more intense executive coaching process)

❖ involvement in honest and developmental feedback processes

❖ a developmental approach to identifying and promoting performance from within the team or workgroup

❖ fostering and maintaining effective and trusting relationships within teams, between teams and with external stakeholders.

CONCLUSION

Many organisations aspire to achieve a coaching culture where coaching is adopted throughout the organisation and is embedded in meetings, reviews, one-to-one working relationships and team and workgroup processes. There are various pathways to achieving a coaching culture and different

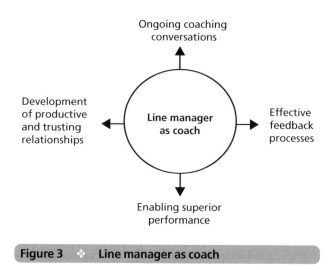

Figure 3 ❖ **Line manager as coach**

organisations may adopt a structured and centralised approach or an emergent and organic approach to the introduction and management of coaching. Organisations that seek to achieve a coaching culture have to overcome a number of obstacles, specifically the attitude, support and confidence shown by line managers as well as variable levels of top management support and the prevalence of a 'command and control' management style. Time, workload and resource constraints are further challenges that must be overcome.

The benefits offered by a coaching culture are considerable and include: the opportunity to develop a people-centred culture; the prospect of fostering more effective relationships within the work environment; and an increase in confidence levels, both for managers and for individuals. However, the requirement for all managers to fulfil a 'manager as coach' role may be problematic. And the aspiration for all managers to be able to develop the full range of skills and techniques that might be expected from an external or internal specialist coach is unrealistic and inappropriate. The role of 'manager as coach' is more effectively articulated as one of 'management style' that is characterised by: regular coaching conversations; effective feedback processes; the encouragement of superior performance; and the development of productive and trusting relationships in the workplace.

These insights were generated by those who already have a commitment towards coaching and management development. Those involved in coaching at work have, so far, not assessed these issues from the perspective of line managers themselves. This issue is addressed in the next chapter.

CHARACTERISTICS OF A COACHING STYLE OF MANAGEMENT – THE LINE MANAGER SURVEY

3

CHAPTER SUMMARY

❖ The CIPD *Managing at the Sharp End* survey was developed to enable a robust understanding of the manager as coach issues from the perspective of line managers. It was completed online by more than 500 managers from public, private and not-for-profit organisations during a five-week period in December 2008 and January 2009.

❖ Survey responses enabled the development of a two-stage model of coaching characteristics that make up a coaching style of management: *primary coaching characteristics* and *mature coaching characteristics*.

❖ Primary coaching characteristics comprise: a development orientation; a performance orientation; effective feedback processes; and successful planning and goal-setting activities.

❖ Mature coaching characteristics, which are also associated with a participative style of management, include: using ideas from team members; powerful questioning; team-based problem-solving; and shared decision-making.

❖ Line managers identify time constraints as the most significant barrier to achieving a coaching style of management. In addition, organisation culture, a perceived lack of skills and a lack of confidence to deal with difficult people can inhibit a coaching style of management.

INTRODUCTION

Chapters 1 and 2 of this report highlighted how coaching is increasingly seen as a way by which organisations and individuals can develop the skills and qualities needed to achieve and sustain competitive advantage, whatever the economic and environmental circumstances they find themselves having to cope with. Where organisations aspire to develop a coaching culture there are implications for the role of line managers. Very little systematic research has been undertaken into the implications for line managers 'at the sharp end'. This forms the focus of the next two chapters.

No consensus has yet emerged about whether 'the line manager as coach' is a feasible or desirable ambition. CIPD research (CIPD 2008a) as well as data from the USA (BlessingWhite 2008) have suggested that there may be a gap between organisational aspirations and 'talk' about 'the line manager as coach' and the daily realities and challenges faced by line managers and those who work for them. Line managers have many different roles: they have to cope with competing

priorities; their objectives can change without warning; and they face increasing time and resource constraints. In this context, the additional demands of the 'line manager as coach' role may be unwelcome (Hutchinson and Purcell 2007; BlessingWhite 2008).

The experiences of many (but not all) of the coaching specialists and HR professionals involved in the *Coaching at the Sharp End* project, whose organisations have gone some way towards a coaching culture (see Chapter 2), lend support to the view that the expectation that managers can fulfil all the expectations of a 'specialist' coaching role may be unrealistic; rather, a 'coaching style of management' may be more appropriate.

The third part of this research examined this issue, focusing specifically on the perspective of line managers themselves, their attitudes and perceptions towards the behaviours associated with a coaching style of management, and the individual and organisational factors that might inhibit or facilitate coaching at work.

A *Managing at the Sharp End* questionnaire was developed for this purpose. A description of the survey questions is included in Appendix 2.

THE MANAGING AT THE SHARP END SURVEY

Although many questionnaires and inventories about coaching have been developed and used over the last ten years, these have tended to focus on the skills and qualities of specialised coaches. Less attention has been paid to the perspective of line managers, so it was necessary to develop a new survey instrument specifically aimed at examining a coaching style of management. The design process took account of a number of issues, which are outlined in Box 1.

BOX 1: QUESTIONNAIRE DESIGN PRINCIPLES

A number of key issues underpinned the design of the questionnaire. First, an acknowledgement that line managers may not all agree about the value of coaching and its relevance to them. Some managers may be convinced of the benefits and make use of a range of coaching behaviours as part of their management style. However, others may be 'agnostic' at best and some are likely to be hostile or sceptical to the idea. A 'coaching questionnaire' is unlikely to be completed by 'coaching sceptics'. Second, managers have limited time for questionnaires and rarely appreciate additional paperwork; withdrawal or refusal rates for long questionnaires are high. Third, line managers may view (or 'rate') their own patterns of behaviour 'in general terms' more positively than others might do.

To maximise participation in the questionnaire, the design incorporated the following principles:

❖ The word 'coaching' was not used in the survey; its title and language focused on 'managing at the sharp end'.

❖ The survey was designed to be completed in ten minutes.

❖ The survey was designed and published to be completed online through a secure Internet web link.

❖ Line manager respondents were asked to reflect on behaviours during the previous three-month period, rather than to reflect on their 'general behaviour'.

KEY FEATURES OF THE DATA

A summary of the survey responses is provided in Appendix 2. In total there were 521 eligible responses, which are divided almost equally between male and female managers (52%, 48%).

Other features of the questionnaire respondents are shown in Table 4. About one in ten respondents describe themselves as a senior or board-level manager and the remaining respondents are fairly evenly spread between middle managers and first-line managers. Nearly one-fifth of the respondents have been in their current post for less than a year and just over half of them have been in post between one and five years. Almost half of the line managers in our survey sample (46.3%) report that they have no management qualification.

Table 4: Characteristics of survey respondents

Gender	All responses (%) n = 521	Private sector (%) n = 261	Public sector (%) n = 174	Not-for-profit sector (%) n = 42	Sector unknown (%) n = 44
Male	52	72	30	36	39
Female	48	28	70	64	61
Age					
Under 25 years	2	1	2	2	2
25–35 years	18	14	22	36	9
35–44 years	33	39	31	24	21
45–54 years	33	35	29	29	50
55–64 years	13	12	16	10	16
Over 64 years	1	0	1	0	2
Level in hierarchy					
First-line manager	42	38	58	26	23
Middle manager	47	49	40	64	55
Top-level/ board manager	11	13	3	10	23
Length of time in current position					
Under 3 months	3	3	3	0	2
3 months – 1 year	15	14	17	24	2
1–5 years	51	51	46	52	75
Over 5 years	31	32	33	24	21
Qualifications					
None	46	39	66	33	23
NVQ (levels 2–4)	17	17	13	17	30
Other business qualification	37	44	21	50	48

IDENTIFYING AND ASSESSING COACHING CHARACTERISTICS

The insights of participants in the Coaching at Work discussion groups and the interview organisations (see Chapter 2) provided a useful starting point when identifying the questions about a coaching style of management to be incorporated in the questionnaire. The behaviours and qualities that they identified were:

❖ engaging in a productive dialogue with team members (listening, questioning, a development orientation, and so on)

❖ facilitating effective feedback processes

❖ developing trusting relationships and rapport

❖ encouraging superior performance (a performance orientation).

Existing published questionnaires and lists relating to coaching styles, behaviours and characteristics were also consulted. These are summarised and paraphrased in Appendix 4.

Features from these published inventories as well as the insights from practitioners (see Chapter 2) provided a useful basis to devise an initial set of 12 survey questions for the *Managing at the Sharp End* survey associated with 'a coaching style of management' and these are shown in Table 5.

Table 5: Characteristics of a coaching style of management

Characteristic	Questionnaire item
Development orientation	I have helped them all to develop themselves as individuals. I actively help them all find and get training/learning to improve their performance and skills.
Performance orientation	I am very good at observing their work to guide my management of them.
Planning and goal-setting	I am very good at helping them all to express their own action plans.
Engagement with dialogue	The time I spend helping them is not valued by any of them.* I ask questions of all of them rather than providing solutions.
Mutual support	If any of them has a good idea, I always use it. I give them all a good share in the decision-making. I want them all to be able to solve problems for themselves.
Effective feedback	I am very conscientious in giving them all feedback on their work – positive and negative. I find it difficult to raise performance shortfalls directly and promptly with all the people I manage.*
Effective listening	Whenever I meet them I spend more time listening than questioning.

* Item asked as a 'negative', so 'reverse coding' was applied when the questionnaire data were analysed.

A summary of the responses to these different survey questions is shown in Table 6.

Table 6: Coaching characteristics	
Think about your behaviour in the last 3 months with the people you manage. Please choose the appropriate response for each item: 'all of the time' (3); 'most of the time' (2); 'some of the time' (1); 'none of the time' (0).	Average rating (rating of 3 is high) n = 521
I am very conscientious in giving them all feedback on their work – positive and negative.	2.55
The time I spend helping them is not valued by any of them.*	2.49
I want them all to be able to solve problems for themselves.	2.48
I find it difficult to raise their performance shortfalls directly and promptly with all the people I manage.*	2.36
If any of them has a good idea, I always use it.	2.13
I actively help them all find and get training/learning to improve their performance and skills.	2.05
Whenever I meet them I spend more time listening than questioning.	1.91
I give them all a good share of the decision-making.	1.88
I am very good at observing their work to guide my management of them.	1.88
I am very good at helping them all to express their own action plans.	1.79
I have helped them all develop themselves as individuals.	1.80
I ask questions of all of them rather than providing solutions.	1.65

* Scoring reversed for this negatively expressed item.

To analyse the data more meaningfully it was important to assess the extent to which the pattern of responses to the survey provide some confidence that these questions taken together constitute a consistent reflection of a coaching style of management. A statistical factor analysis test was undertaken to assess this (see Appendix 3). A number of interesting insights arose from this procedure, in particular the existence of two discrete 'clusters' of characteristics. The first cluster to emerge from the analysis relates to five of the survey questions, which have been called primary coaching characteristics (see Figure 4).

Primary coaching characteristics

❖ I have helped them all develop themselves as individuals.

❖ I am very good at observing their work to guide my management of them.

❖ I am very good at helping them all to express their own action plans.

❖ I actively help them all find and get training/learning to improve their performance and skills.

❖ I am very conscientious in giving them all feedback on their work – positive and negative.

A second cluster of questions was also evident from the analysis, referred to here as 'mature coaching characteristics', comprised from the following four survey questions (see Figure 5).

Mature coaching characteristics

❖ I ask questions of all of them rather than providing solutions.

❖ I give them all a good share of the decision-making.

❖ If any of them has a good idea, I always use it.

❖ I want them all to be able to solve problems for themselves.

A TWO-STAGE MODEL OF A COACHING STYLE OF MANAGEMENT

Key features of the primary coaching characteristics identified here are a development orientation and a performance orientation as well as effective feedback and planning and goal-setting skills.

In addition to these primary coaching characteristics, there are further characteristics that have been called mature coaching characteristics, which include: powerful questioning; using

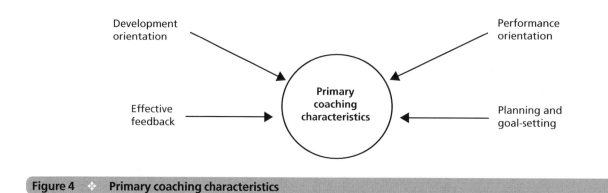

ideas; shared decision-making; and encouraging problem-solving (see Figure 5). The data suggest that these mature coaching characteristics are more disparate, however, and they lack a clear and coherent relationship with each other. This may reflect the way in which these mature features of a coaching style of management are associated with a participative style of management. For example, whereas primary-level questioning would form an important feature of effective feedback skills, powerful questioning focuses on empowering team members to identify potential solutions to problems for themselves. In addition, mature coaching is characterised by a focus on affirming and using good ideas offered by team members, giving them a share in the decision-making and encouraging

an approach where they solve problems for themselves – all of which may be associated with what is often referred to as a 'participative style of management'.

Every organisation is different, but the analysis of survey responses suggests that organisations that encourage managers to develop and use primary coaching skills will, over time, develop a less directive management style as mature coaching characteristics reflect a more participative approach to management. The Southern Railway case study included here provides an example of this process as part of a wider set of organisational changes.

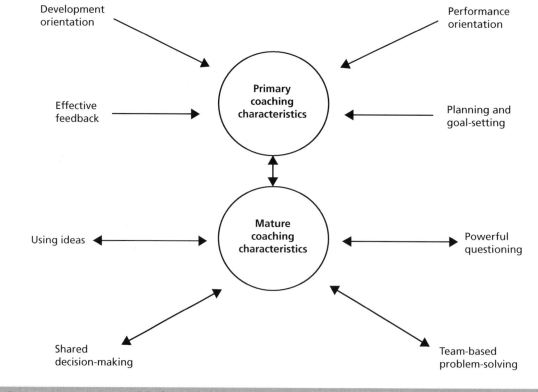

Figure 5 ❖ **A two-stage model of coaching at the sharp end**

CASE STUDY: EMPOWERING PEOPLE THROUGH COACHING – SOUTHERN RAILWAY

The background

Southern Railway is a train operating company operating a mix of suburban commuter and mainline routes between London and England's south-east coast as well as the prestigious Gatwick Express non-stop rail service between London Victoria and Gatwick Airport. Around 4,200 people work for Southern; its staff manage over 160 stations and maintain a fleet of more than 300 trains, which run seven days a week on a nearly 24/7 basis. The company won the southern England rail franchise from Connex in 2001. At that point morale was low, performance was poor and management style was dominated by a command and control, directive approach. A key issue for Southern was to initiate an organisation-wide change process embracing all those involved in driving the trains, selling the tickets and maintaining and cleaning the train fleet to achieve the delivery of a customer-focused high-quality service for passengers.

In line with other train operating companies many of the management staff at Southern have been with the company and its predecessor organisations for many years. Historically they were promoted on the basis of their technical ability rather than for their people skills. A key issue for Zoey Hudson, Southern's Leadership and Behavioural Development Manager, was to find a way to 'give these managers a toolkit of how to manage and to give them the people skills and confidence to deal with people'.

An organic and emergent approach to coaching

Coaching has been introduced in an incremental and organic way at Southern. Since 2005 about 20 people each year have undertaken an intensive one-year accredited coaching course. Each of those people has then gone on to coach three to four others within Southern and so the effect of coaching has gradually 'spread out'. Over the years a robust internal coaching service has been built and by mid-2009 there will be more than 80 qualified coaches, of whom several are executive-level managers. A system of coaching supervision is also being developed to ensure appropriate support for the coaches themselves and to enable a process of continuous reflection and enhancement of the internal coaching provision.

Southern does not encourage line managers who are trained as coaches to undertake formal coaching with members of their own teams, nor indeed with anyone in the same functional area of the business. A fundamental feature of the Southern approach is the encouragement of a confidential professional relationship between the coach and the 'coachee'. Coaching is developmental rather than 'remedial' and there is a separation of coaching processes from the line management relationship so that 'boundary issues' do not arise and a 'neutral power zone' can be maintained.

Coaching and the line manager

Although Southern's coaches do not engage in any formal coaching with members of their own teams, coaching skills for managers have been introduced into general management training and development programmes. At Southern the development of this coaching style of management means that people can move beyond seeing feedback as focusing on things that people are doing wrong and encourage them instead to engage in a dialogue around people's strengths to build on them and maximise effectiveness. Creating two-way rapport, developing quality development plans, listening more and using incisive questions are further skills that are encouraged as part of the less directive management style.

The incremental and emergent approach taken at Southern has enabled coaching to become gradually embedded. The need to have leaders who coach and facilitate their people to improve what is delivered to passengers is accepted throughout the organisation. The newly introduced appraisal system, for example, has been developed around the requirement for a coaching and engaging style of leadership. All appraisers have been trained in the new system, which includes what is, in effect, a coaching skills module to enable them to conduct an appraisal in a coaching style.

Organisational outcomes

Coaching has had an important 'informal' impact on people at all levels at Southern, particularly in moving the organisation away from its old command and control culture. It is no longer expected that managers should have the answer to everything. Instead a developmental and empowering approach to draw on the skills and knowledge of team members is being established. Zoey comments that, 'Coaching has brought this organisation to a position where people at all levels are able to feel more empowered about the decisions they make on a day-to-day basis.' Anecdotally she hears that managers at all levels are adopting new approaches, for example, facilitating meetings in a coaching style rather than coming along with all the agenda laid out and all the answers for their people ready in advance.

Hard data about the impact of coaching is also becoming available. In 2008 a Gallup business impact survey showed that staff engagement at Southern was significantly improved; interestingly, engagement among the teams of those who had been trained as coaches was even higher than for the rest of the organisation.

Other Southern achievements include: improved train performance and train reliability; best ever customer service survey results; and reduced levels of staff absence. Coaching is part of a wider package of change initiatives at Southern but the business now accepts the important role it plays. A coaching steering group has been established and its members include senior managers from the engineering, operations and commercial functions as well as the HR director. Coaching is now too important to be an HR initiative; it is owned, driven and valued by the business.

WHO COACHES AT WORK?

Developing a model of a coaching style of management provides a useful step forward in understanding coaching at the sharp end. It is also necessary to assess the extent to which both primary coaching characteristics and mature coaching characteristics were reported by the line managers who responded to the survey. Analysis of the responses to these questions indicates that these characteristics are not associated with any particular group within the data (defined, for example, by age, experience or gender), although there is a correlation between seniority (first-line manager, middle manager, top-level/board manager) and mature coaching characteristics.

This suggests that all managers have the potential to develop and implement a coaching style of management.

The responses to another of the survey questions shed further light on this. Coaching and HR specialists (see Chapter 2) identified the importance of managers' willingness to respond flexibly to the different development and performance priorities of individuals within their team if a coaching style of management is to be realised. The survey examined this issue (see Appendix 2) and asked respondents to reflect on the approach that underpinned their personal approach to managing their staff. Over 64% of respondents report that they take account of individual differences in the way that they manage their staff, suggesting a good level of flexibility and responsiveness by managers in response to the different needs of the members of their teams and that most, but not all, managers have the potential to develop and implement a coaching style of management.

Further analysis, taking into account levels of seniority (first-line manager, middle manager or top-level/board manager) indicates that first-line managers respond more frequently to the 'treat them the same' response options; middle managers, by contrast, respond more frequently to the 'treat them differently' options. Therefore, although the data suggest that most managers have the potential to develop and make use of a coaching style of management, it seems that first-line managers may be less likely to feel able to exhibit the flexibility and responsiveness required.

The ability of first-line managers to respond in a flexible way to the development needs of their staff is highlighted here as a key issue for organisations that wish to develop a coaching culture.

Organisations must also be aware of, and tackle where appropriate, any further 'barriers' that inhibit the development of a coaching style of management. The survey provided the opportunity for managers to highlight what they saw as the barriers and these are considered in the next section.

BARRIERS TO A COACHING STYLE OF MANAGEMENT

Three important obstacles to a coaching style of management were identified by HR and coaching practitioners (see Chapter 2): organisational culture; a lack of clarity about coaching styles and expectations; and time and resource constraints. The line manager survey also examined these issues.

First, respondents were asked:

❖ In an ideal world, would you have liked to have done more or less of this type of (coaching) work with your team?

Over half of the sample (56%) responded 'more' and the remaining 44% responded 'neither, it has been just right'. A series of supplementary items were offered to those respondents who replied that they would like to do more in order to identify what they saw as barriers to coaching.

The responses are shown in Table 7. Concern about the time implications of coaching, highlighted in Chapter 2, was by far the most significant barrier identified by the questionnaire respondents. The other items that were noteworthy relate to organisational culture ('it's not the style in our organisation') as well as issues of confidence to deal with difficult people and a perceived lack of skills.

Table 7: Barriers to coaching	
Barrier	Mean rating (out of 100) n = 284
I haven't the time.	62
It's not the style in our organisation.	10
They are difficult people.	9
I lack the skills.	6
I don't know where to start.	4
It's not my style.	3
I haven't got the patience.	2
It's not part of my job.	2
There's no reward for me.	2
My staff would leave	1

The most frequently cited issues must be tackled if an organisation-wide coaching culture is to be achieved and line managers are to feel able to develop a coaching style of management in a consistent way. The analysis does show a strong correlation between two of the barriers: 'I don't know where to start' and 'I lack the skills'. In addition, a weaker link is also evident with these two barriers and 'they are difficult people'. These findings indicate that organisational support for managers, to develop their levels of skill, confidence to cope with 'difficult people' and knowledge about coaching, is a priority if a coaching culture is to become a reality.

CONCLUSION

The two-stage model of coaching at the sharp end presented here highlights important implications for organisations if a coaching culture is to be achieved. First, it is important to recognise that 'the manager as a coach' role cannot be a full substitute for specialised coaching activities and relationships. Instead, it is important to give clarity to managers about behaviours that comprise 'a coaching style of management'. The exact mix of behaviours, tools and techniques will vary somewhat in different organisational situations, cultures and contexts, but the two-stage model of coaching characteristics developed here provides a useful starting point for organisations wanting to develop a coaching style of management:

- primary coaching characteristics:
  - a development orientation
  - a performance orientation
  - planning and goal-setting skills
  - feedback skills

- mature coaching characteristics:
  - powerful questioning
  - using ideas
  - shared decision-making
  - team-based problem-solving.

The survey responses confirm that a coaching style of management is associated with an approach that is more participative and developmental. A brief assessment of the barriers to coaching in organisations also suggests that different factors will influence the extent to which a coaching style of management is achievable. These are considered in more detail in Chapter 4.

FACTORS AFFECTING A COACHING STYLE OF MANAGEMENT

CHAPTER SUMMARY

✤ The *Managing at the Sharp End* survey examined in more detail four factors that may affect a coaching style of management: manager self-confidence; the work and task environment; manager–team relationships; and development and support offered to managers.

✤ The survey data indicate that levels of manager self-confidence are closely associated with coaching characteristics. It is not possible to say which comes first. It is likely that the development of a coaching culture leads to increased levels of self-confidence in managers, although increased self-confidence is also a prerequisite for a manager to engage in a coaching style of management.

✤ The survey suggests that the overall work and task environment within which managers and their teams operate is not a factor that will, of itself, diminish or enhance the chances of achieving a coaching culture. However, mature coaching characteristics are positively associated with levels of seniority in the organisation. This suggests that the operational constraints experienced by first-line managers who are closer to 'the sharp end' may inhibit a coaching style of management.

✤ Our analysis indicates that a coaching style of management is more likely in organisations that also foster effective team relationships and provide opportunities for managers to develop their level of self-confidence.

✤ The survey shows that most managers appreciate the value of a range of formal and informal training and support avenues in the development of their management approach. Importantly, attitudes towards training and support are correlated with both primary and mature coaching characteristics. Training and support are necessary to foster a coaching style of management, but the development of coaching characteristics is also likely to lead to a greater commitment to learning and development more generally.

✤ No evidence is found of an association between the age, gender, qualifications or length of experience of managers with variables such as manager self-confidence, manager–team relationships or attitudes towards training and support. In other words, all managers have an equal chance of being able to develop these qualities and characteristics.

INTRODUCTION

Chapter 3 introduced a two-stage model of a coaching style of management that emerged from analysis of the *Managing at the Sharp End* survey. It also highlighted how managers, HR professionals and coaching specialists need to be aware of the barriers that can inhibit the development of a coaching culture. This chapter builds on this initial assessment and examines in depth some of the issues that affect coaching at the sharp end, both inhibitors and facilitators.

COACHING AT THE SHARP END: INFLUENCING FACTORS

A number of influences affecting a coaching culture were identified by the interview and discussion group participants (see Chapter 2). Research into coaching and into the role of line managers in learning, training and development also highlights the importance of encouraging 'facilitating factors' and tackling inhibitors to coaching (Clutterbuck and Megginson 2005; Hutchinson and Purcell 2007; BlessingWhite

2008). From this basis a provisional model of the factors that affect coaching at the sharp end was derived (see Figure 6); the *Managing at the Sharp End* survey provided the opportunity to test these. Specifically, the survey examined four factors:

❖ manager self-confidence

❖ work and task environment

❖ manager–team relationships

❖ development and support for managers.

MANAGER SELF-CONFIDENCE

Confidence (or a lack of it) emerged as an important issue from both HR and coaching practitioners (see Chapter 2) as well as from the initial assessment of barriers to coaching indicated from the survey responses (see Chapter 3). To understand more about the relationship between coaching characteristics and self-confidence, the survey included a number of measures related to 'self-efficacy'. These have been developed to detect the confidence that an individual has in their ability to cope and successfully complete tasks. The survey made use of six questions to assess manager confidence/self-efficacy (Rigotti et al 2008):

❖ I can remain calm when facing difficulties in my job because I can rely on my abilities.

❖ When I am confronted with a problem in my job I can usually find several solutions.

❖ Whatever comes my way in my job I can usually handle it.

❖ My past experiences in my job have prepared me well for my occupational future.

❖ I meet the goals that I set for myself in my job.

❖ I feel prepared for most of the demands in my job.

Analysis of the survey responses shows no correlation between characteristics such as age, gender or management qualifications and this group of 'self-confidence' questions. In other words, a young, female manager with or without qualifications is just as likely to report high (or low) levels of self-confidence as an older male colleague who has been in his post for a significant period of time. However, the analysis does show a strong link between manager self-confidence with primary coaching characteristics as well as a weaker link with mature coaching characteristics (see Appendix 3). Manager self-confidence is, therefore, an important influence on a coaching style of management. It is not possible to determine whether developing coaching characteristics leads to self-confidence or whether self-confidence is a necessary first step towards coaching behaviours. Most probably both are true, which makes it all the more important that organisations that seek to develop a coaching culture should ensure sufficient support and development to line managers to enable them to develop in both of these important areas.

THE WORK AND TASK ENVIRONMENT

In addition to self-confidence issues it is likely that coaching behaviours may also be influenced by the nature of the environment and context in which management takes place (Clutterbuck and Megginson 2005; Hutchinson and Purcell 2007). Three features of the *Managing at the Sharp End* questionnaire enabled this feature to be assessed:

❖ the respondent's position in the organisational hierarchy (first-line manager; middle manager; top manager/board manager)

❖ autonomy levels within the workgroup – the extent to which it is expected that people can take responsibility for their own work and determine, within agreed limits, how they will achieve their objectives

❖ the task variety involved in the work of their team – the extent to which work patterns and methods are prescribed and standardised, leaving little room for manoeuvre for individuals or their managers.

A good level of association was seen between seniority and mature coaching characteristics. This may indicate that senior managers have more opportunity to exercise the behaviours associated with this characteristic with their (middle management) direct reports, than those who are closer to 'the sharp end'.

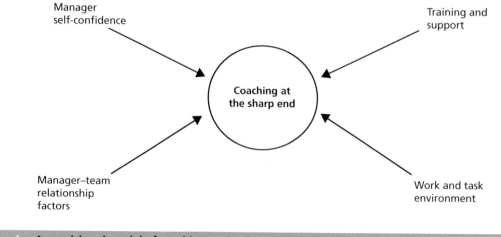

Figure 6 ❖ **A provisional model of coaching at the sharp end**

In addition, to examine the work and task environment, the *Managing at the Sharp End* questionnaire drew on influential research that has explored the impact of situational factors (including task variety and autonomy) on the behaviour of managers and leaders (Kerr and Jermier 1978; Jermier and Kerr 1997). The results indicate that, although the work and task environment is important, these factors are not significant for the development of a coaching style of management. This means that organisations of different types and with different approaches to job design can benefit from the development of a coaching culture. However, the data also suggest that constraints on managers in the lower positions in the hierarchy may limit the extent to which they can fully develop a coaching style of management.

MANAGER–TEAM RELATIONSHIPS

Another factor in the coaching equation, highlighted particularly by HR and coaching practitioners (see Chapter 2), is the quality of relationships within the organisation, particularly between members of workgroups and their manager. Effective coaching requires a trusting relationship to be established between those involved in the process. The *Managing at the Sharp End* survey focused on the perspective of line managers towards their team members. The six survey statements were:

❖ I admire their professional skills.

❖ I respect their knowledge and competence on the job.

❖ I work for them beyond what is specified in their job description.

❖ I am willing to apply extra effort to further their interests.

❖ I do not mind working hard for them.

❖ I am impressed with their knowledge of their job.

As with levels of manager self-confidence, analysis of the survey responses indicates that the quality of manager–team relationships is not influenced by a person's age, seniority, gender or length of experience as a manager. Male or female managers with or without a senior position in the management hierarchy, management qualifications and with different patterns of experience are all just as likely (or unlikely) to be able to engage in productive working relationships with members of their teams. In addition, the analysis of the survey data shows a strong correlation between manager–team relationships and with levels of manager self-confidence.

More importantly for this analysis, the survey responses indicate a good level of correlation with primary coaching characteristics as well as a correlation (albeit less strong) with mature coaching characteristics. Again, it is not possible to determine whether coaching causes better manager–team relationships or whether good relationships form the basis from which coaching behaviours by line managers can thrive; indeed both may be true. However, the clear message for those who wish to promote a coaching culture is to ensure that the background factors such as organisational culture and team relationships are addressed if a coaching style of management is to be achieved. The VT Group case study provides an example of how coaching has formed a major part in improving relationships within teams, within different business functions, and with suppliers and customers.

CASE STUDY: DEVELOPING A PERFORMANCE-LED COACHING CULTURE – VT GROUP PLC

The background

The VT Group is a leading defence and support services company which, in addition to its well-known ship-building business, operates across a wide range of markets providing engineering and other services to governments and large organisations throughout the world. VT employs over 14,000 people and operates in a startling array of market sectors including defence, logistics, communications, education and training. The group has over 100 offices in the UK and has extensive operations in the USA as well as in South America, Europe, Asia and the Pacific and Atlantic Oceans.

VT's vision is to develop the organisation to build on its traditional engineering strengths to become the number one international government services group. In 2006 the top team recognised that achieving this vision would require a step-change in the development and leadership of people. Paul Lester, CEO, was keen to 'improve performance a couple of notches' (a phrase that is often used in VT), and Jo Robbins, HR Director, also recognised the need to 'shift the organisation culture from command and control in our ship-building days to a more modern participative style'. Their Coaching for High Performance Programme was initiated as part of the change process.

Coaching for high performance

VT took a 'top–down' approach to the introduction of a coaching culture. An ambitious programme of development for senior executives was launched in November 2006 and 45 executives from across VT's five business units committed to undertake a specially developed 'VT Henley Certificate in Coaching' programme. The second stage began in April 2007 and a further tier of 120 managers undertook a shortened and more practical programme, 'Coaching for High Performance', which was developed by VT in collaboration with Roffey Park. It is intended that this process will continue to include a further 500 managers throughout the organisation.

A key driver for VT's approach is its commitment to develop a 'performance-led coaching culture'. Coaching is now seen as something that forms part of each manager's work and is directly connected with business priorities. The emphasis is on enabling better performance through the application of simple and practical techniques and behaviours, without necessarily engaging all of the time in 'formal coaching sessions'.

The organisation is working hard at embedding coaching and ensuring that all managers are clear about why coaching is important to VT and what is expected of them. They are encouraged to make use of important behaviours and qualities that make up a coaching style of management, such as giving and receiving feedback, building rapport and listening. They are introduced to the GROW model of performance coaching (Alexander and Renshaw 2005) and the DELACT model of more directive coaching (see, for example, Holbeche 2005). 'Master classes' to further develop specific aspects of their coaching expertise are currently being planned.

Embedding the coaching culture

Michael Staunton, Executive Development and Succession Planning Director, who has spear-headed coaching in the group, highlights how VT have tackled the issue of embedding its coaching culture: first, through its top–down approach, which has led to coaching being actively sponsored by the board and executives, all of whom have participated in the programme, and which is now being cascaded throughout the organisation; second, by building a critical mass of 'coaching-enabled' managers focused on 'a performance-led coaching culture and common language'; third, encouraging managers to spend time with their subordinates regularly and, when required, to improve individual and team performance; and finally, integrating coaching development with other forms of talent management and succession planning.

The VT approach is to communicate clearly that coaching is not additional to a manager's day job but is part of every manager's day-to-day management style. Michael Staunton reminds them that coaching outcomes can sometimes be achieved through 'a few minutes here, a few minutes there'. He stresses that coaching can give managers more time because: 'If your team members need your help less because they are more capable, then time is less of an issue.'

VT take a very public approach to their commitment to coaching, both within the organisation and when working with customer and partner organisations. Michael Staunton puts it like this: 'If you are joining the company there's a promise that you are going to be in a coaching environment and you are going to be coached rather than managed in a traditional, top–down way. If you're working with us as a customer then you know that we've got that coaching mindset; you're going to be treated fairly to achieve shared goals.'

Organisational outcomes

In the two years since the launch of the 'coaching for high performance' initiative, VT has posted some impressive results. Both revenues and profits have increased and other, 'softer' areas of business effectiveness have shown improvement. Talented executives are reaffirming their desire to remain within the VT Group and business relationships with customers and partner organisations are improving – in some cases enabling VT managers to engage in 'buddy coaching' relationships with key contacts in partner organisations.

Paul Lester, the CEO, comments: 'The benefits are starting to come through. I can see much more confidence in the management team.' For Michael Staunton, the coaching culture is increasingly helping the organisation to get the best out of people at all levels, whether they are experienced managers, technical experts, new graduates or apprentices, by encouraging greater personal responsibility and autonomy and helping those who previously worked in 'business silos' to feel confident to work across divisions and business units.

DEVELOPMENT AND SUPPORT FOR LINE MANAGERS

Team relationships and levels of managers' self-confidence are clear influences on coaching as a style of management. Another issue identified by participants in the *Coaching at the Sharp End* interviews (see Chapter 2) was the development and support needed for line managers. Research and practice relating to learning and training in the workplace has highlighted the limitations of relying on instructor-led training provision for managers. Additionally, a range of work-based formal and informal methods of development are important as part of a development and support package for managers (Hutchinson and Purcell 2007; CIPD 2004; CIPD 2008d). Five survey questions were included to address these issues. Line managers were asked 'in an ideal world' whether they would find the following opportunities helpful to develop their coaching behaviours:

❖ in-house training course

❖ external training course

❖ being given space to learn by trial and error

❖ advice and guidance from a senior manager/mentor

❖   one-to-one coaching from their manager.

The frequency findings (see Table 8) indicate almost no variation in preference for different types of learning and support activities, regardless of the sector background of respondents. The overall picture is that all types of learning opportunity, formal and informal, are perceived by most managers to be helpful in developing coaching behaviours.

Table 8: In an ideal world, what would be helpful to improve these activities with the people you manage?

In-house training course	Very helpful (%)	Helpful (%)	Not very helpful (%)	Not helpful (%)
All respondents n = 521	29	50	14	7
Public sector n = 174	31	47	16	7
Private sector n = 261	30	52	13	5
Not-for-profit sector n = 42	24	52	17	7
Sector not known n = 44	27	50	11	11
External training course				
All respondents n = 521	18	52	21	8
Public sector n = 174	20	48	22	9
Private sector n = 261	15	56	23	7
Not-for-profit sector n = 42	21	52	21	5
Sector not known n = 44	27	48	9	16
Being given space to learn by trial and error				
All respondents n = 521	20	49	22	9
Public sector n = 174	19	53	20	8
Private sector n = 261	18	45	25	12
Not-for-profit sector n = 42	24	62	12	2
Sector not known n = 44	32	43	23	2

	Very helpful (%)	Helpful (%)	Not very helpful (%)	Not helpful (%)
Advice and guidance from a senior manager/mentor				
All respondents n = 521	33	55	8	4
Public sector n = 174	31	53	12	5
Private sector n = 261	35	55	6	4
Not-for-profit sector n = 42	29	60	7	5
Sector not known n = 44	39	52	2	7
One-to-one coaching from my manager				
All respondents n = 521	25	49	17	9
Public sector n = 174	20	49	20	12
Private sector n = 261	28	49	17	6
Not-for-profit sector n = 42	19	45	24	12
Sector not known n = 44	32	55	7	7

Most importantly, the analysis confirms a link between the reported helpfulness of different training and support opportunities with both primary and mature coaching characteristics, confirming the views expressed in the organisational interviews. Training and support, it seems, is an 'input factor' for the development of a coaching style of management. In addition, as managers adopt coaching characteristics, they are more likely to appreciate the value of different learning and support opportunities.

FACTORS AFFECTING A COACHING STYLE OF MANAGEMENT

Chapter 3 of this report identified patterns of coaching characteristics that make up a coaching style of management and presented a model that comprises both primary coaching characteristics and mature coaching characteristics. This chapter has further assessed the extent to which different individual and organisational factors may affect the extent to

which a coaching culture is possible from the perspective of line managers themselves.

Four key factors have emerged from the analysis (see Figure 7). First, a range of training and support opportunities are perceived to be helpful by line managers to enable them to develop a coaching style of management. Formal training courses have an important role to play but work-based learning opportunities, such as advice and guidance from a senior manager or mentor and the opportunity for one-to-one coaching with their manager, may also be valuable.

Second, levels of management self-confidence are shown to be an important influence on a coaching style of management. Managers need to feel confident in themselves to demonstrate coaching characteristics. At the same time, engagement with a coaching style of management may also lead to enhanced levels of a manager's self-confidence. No relationship is discernible between self-confidence and perceptions of the helpfulness of different training and support methods, suggesting that there is 'no one right way' through which levels of self-confidence can be developed.

Third, although the reliability of these questions is less strong than for other parts of the survey, the nature of the work and task relationship is not significant for the development of coaching characteristics. Coaching behaviours, appropriately 'tailored', can be just as appropriate where levels of task variety are low and work is standardised and routine as when higher levels of worker autonomy feature as an aspect of job design.

Fourth, relationships between managers and their team members is an important influence on the extent to which a coaching style of management is likely to be possible. Both primary and mature coaching characteristics are correlated with relationships between leaders and their team members. This is a factor that may influence coaching behaviours and also may be an outcome of the development of a coaching culture. Relationships between managers and their team members are also positively correlated with levels of self-confidence, indicating that these are important interrelated factors.

CONCLUSION

The model of coaching at the sharp end presented here indicates that organisations that are serious about developing a coaching culture need to adopt an integrated package of individual, team and organisation development processes to ensure:

❖ appropriately devised and tailored training and support interventions to enable managers to develop their primary and more mature coaching capabilities

❖ teamworking and relationships between managers and their team members

❖ levels of manager self-confidence.

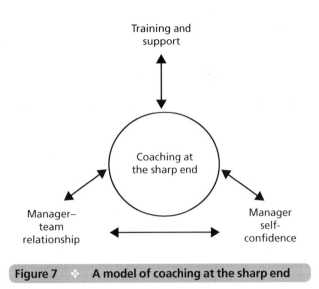

Figure 7 ❖ **A model of coaching at the sharp end**

The model indicates that coaching at the sharp end can become something of a 'virtuous circle'. Levels of management self-confidence and manager–team relationships are important influences on the development of a coaching style of management. However, as managers are increasingly able to use their coaching skills, so good-quality team relationships and levels of self-confidence are likely to be reinforced and enhanced.

Chapter 5 of this report brings together the analysis from the *Managing at the Sharp End* questionnaire with the insights of the *Coaching at the Sharp End* discussion groups and interview organisations. It examines the most appropriate ways by which organisations can 'move forward' with coaching at the sharp end.

WHERE NOW FOR COACHING AT THE SHARP END?   **5**

CHAPTER SUMMARY

❖ The expectation that line managers can fulfil all the functions of a specialist coach is not realistic and probably not desirable. The manager as coach role is better described as a coaching style of management.

❖ Primary and mature coaching characteristics comprise a coaching style of management and these can form part of the wider development of a participative style of management in organisations.

❖ A coaching style of management is as appropriate for organisations facing the challenges of hostile economic conditions as it is for those enjoying business growth and development.

❖ Successful implementation of coaching at the sharp end requires HR professionals to work with their line management colleagues to diagnose the most effective way forward in implementing and embedding coaching so that it becomes part of 'business as normal'. This involves: giving consistent attention to the time and resource constraints facing all managers, particularly those closest to 'the sharp end'; providing appropriate and relevant training and support; fostering effective teamworking and relationships; and encouraging managers to develop confidence in their coaching capability.

INTRODUCTION

The *Coaching at the Sharp End* project set out to assess the role of the line manager as coach. Line managers are crucial to people management and development and the increasing emphasis on the role of the line manager as coach is part of a wider trend in some organisations towards a coaching culture. This report examines the line manager as coach issues from the perspective of line managers themselves, taking into account the different responsibilities, competing priorities and resource constraints that they have to deal with.

Opinion is divided about the extent to which the line manager as coach idea is feasible, or even desirable. While coaching skills may be part of a manager's 'toolkit' it may be inappropriate to expect them to engage in the deep rapport, high level of confidentiality and 'boundary maintenance' agreements expected from 'formal' coaching relationships. The position adopted here is that the line manager as coach role is better understood as a coaching style of management. As managers adopt a coaching style of management, so their overall approach to management is likely to move away from one characterised as 'command and control' towards a more participative style.

Survey data as well as information from interviews and discussion groups provided the basis from which to examine the skills, behaviours and characteristics that are needed for a coaching style of management. Three important issues emerged from the research. First, there are two elements to a coaching style of management: primary coaching characteristics and mature coaching characteristics. Primary coaching characteristics include a development orientation and a performance orientation as well as engaging in effective feedback processes and successful planning and goal-setting activities with their staff. Mature coaching characteristics, which are also associated with a participative style of management, involve: using ideas from team members; powerful questioning; team-based problem-solving; and shared decision-making.

Second, a coaching style of management is not something that can be achieved in isolation. Training and support is required and managers need to have personal confidence in their abilities. In addition, coaching as a style of management has to be grounded in constructive relationships both within and between teams. Third, time constraints are a serious and significant barrier to 'living out' a coaching style of management. Neither personal factors, such as a manager's age, gender, length of experience or level of qualifications, nor the overall work and task environment within which they work make a significant difference to whether or not managers adopt a coaching style of management. However, mature coaching characteristics are more likely to be achieved by those in more senior positions, who often have more 'discretionary time' and are less caught up in the operational and short-term challenges that pervade life for first-line managers, who are closer to 'the sharp end'.

This chapter examines the implications of these issues. First, it presents a model of coaching at the sharp end, derived from the insights gained from those who participated in the research (see Figure 8). On the basis of this model it considers coaching at the sharp end in the light of the sustained economic downturn in which organisations are now operating. It also assesses the roles and responsibilities of top managers, line managers and HR professionals for organisations that wish to promote coaching as a style of management as part of their strategy to manage the short-term challenges as well as the longer-term issues with which they are faced. This provides the basis for a framework through which those involved in organisations, at all levels of management, can move forward with coaching at the sharp end.

A MODEL OF COACHING AT THE SHARP END

The model of coaching at the sharp end developed here is based on the insights of line managers and HR and coaching professionals who participated in the research project. The model includes three important features. First it takes account of the dual nature of a coaching style of management (see Chapter 3), which are summarised in Table 9.

Table 9: Primary and mature coaching characteristics	
Primary coaching characteristics	Mature coaching characteristics
❖ development orientation	❖ powerful questioning
❖ performance orientation	❖ using ideas
❖ planning and goal-setting skills	❖ shared decision-making
❖ effective feedback skills	❖ team-based problem-solving

Second, the model indicates important influences and outcomes of the development of a coaching style of management at the personal and team levels. These are: training and support; manager–team relationships; and manager self-confidence. These influences enable managers to develop coaching characteristics, but once the process has started a 'virtuous circle' is possible where levels of manager self-confidence, constructive teamwork and a positive outlook towards learning and development are more likely.

Third, the model makes clear that organisational climate and business-wide factors (see Chapter 2) also influence the extent to which a coaching style of management can be achieved (see Figure 9). Senior management ownership of coaching as a business issue and top management role-modelling of coaching characteristics are necessary. In addition, clarity about coaching roles and expectations combined with a clear acceptance of the time and resource constraints on the extent to which managers 'at the sharp end' can develop and sustain coaching characteristics as part of their role are needed.

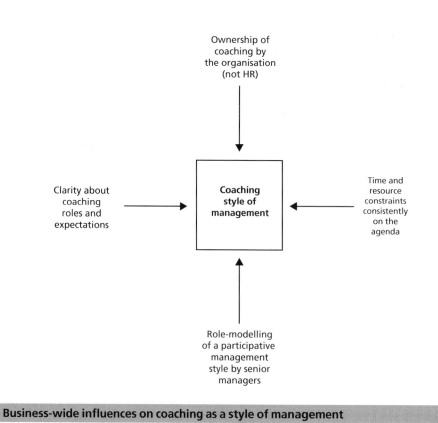

Figure 8 ❖ Business-wide influences on coaching as a style of management

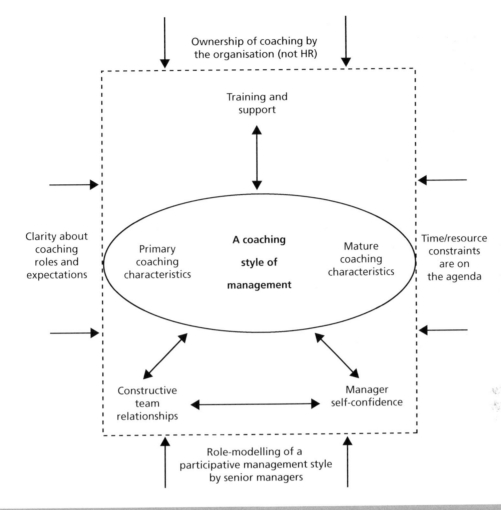

Figure 9 ⋄ **A model of coaching at the sharp end**

COACHING IN ADVERSITY

Organisations in the UK as elsewhere now find that they face difficult economic circumstances and their employees are equally conscious of uncertain labour market conditions. In the past coaching has been promoted as a means of equipping people to cope with organisational growth and individual development. The challenges facing individuals and organisations are now very different. Many organisations face declining revenue growth; customers or suppliers may be seeking to renegotiate contracts; HR budgets are under threat; 'headcount' is in the spotlight and tensions in the employment relationship are surfacing, leading to diminished levels of employee engagement and commitment. Change is occurring in many organisations, although not for reasons that are welcomed by organisations or their stakeholders.

On the one hand, an examination of the consequences of curtailed organisational growth and environmental uncertainty might lead to pessimism about the future of coaching and the role of the line manager as coach. First, there may be a danger of a return to 'macho management' rather than participative management as circumstances change. Headcount reductions can mean that managers and their teams are expected to cope with significant additional work so that time and other resources are even more constrained – both of which are factors that will diminish the extent to which a coaching style

of management is likely. Second, many organisations have not yet developed levels of management capability to cope with 'slimmed down' budgets and headcounts; overconfidence in managers is clearly inappropriate, but overcautious management strategies may be equally unsuitable. Third, new skills are needed to manage relationships with employees in a situation where traditional reward strategies are no longer available and where engagement and commitment will be harder to achieve. Finally, coaching is considered to be a developmental approach where the benefits are achieved over the medium to long term; current economic constraints in organisations can easily lead to a fixation with the short term so that talent management and development issues are neglected.

However, the coaching at the sharp end model presented here also suggests a positive case for coaching at the sharp end 'in adversity'. First, hard economic circumstances emphasise the performance imperative in organisations. The development and retention of high-performers must not be neglected so that sufficient people of good quality will be in place to ensure a head start when economic recovery begins. At the same time a robust and proactive approach is needed to manage poor performance. The research reported here clearly indicates the contribution that a coaching style of management can make to both of these priorities; it is unlikely that a return to directive, command and control approaches will achieve them. Second, coaching of managers by managers can contribute to the development of newer management capabilities that individuals require if they are to make the transition to managing in a slimmed down organisation. Third, employee engagement and commitment are key variables for organisations during difficult times and the *Coaching at the Sharp End* project has shown that a coaching style of management delivers benefits that are manifested in better team relationships, enhanced levels of self-confidence and more general improvements to engagement, flexibility and commitment.

The extent to which a coaching style of management is developed and sustained during the current period of economic insecurity cannot be predicted; the inhibiting and the driving factors may well be finely balanced (see Figure 10). However, the experience of KPMG gives some confidence that a coaching culture can enable organisations to tackle challenging business conditions in a flexible and proactive way.

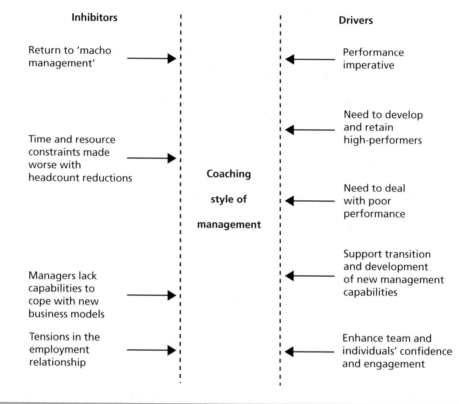

Figure 10 ❖ **Coaching at the sharp end – where now?**

CASE STUDY: COACHING AND FLEXIBILITY IN CHANGING CIRCUMSTANCES – KPMG

The background

KPMG is a leading provider of professional audit, tax, financial and risk advisory services. KPMG in the UK has over 10,000 partners and staff working in 22 offices. In 2008–09, KPMG in the UK, Germany, Switzerland, Spain and Belgium merged to form KPMG Europe LLP. This innovative step, the first in the accountancy profession, was part of KPMG's vision to provide integrated audit, tax and advisory services for international clients on a pan-European basis. Delivering this ambition means that KPMG has to recruit and retain the best talent and must invest in their development to ensure that the talent needed to support long-term success is available.

KPMG has invested in coaching over a number of years. Coaching was first developed in response to a retention issue six or more years ago, but the position and purpose of coaching has evolved over time and, in addition to being part of the organisation's talent retention and career management strategy, coaching is also seen as a key part of performance management.

A team of full-time internal coaches provide the bedrock of coaching at KPMG; their role is to provide one-to-one coaching for individuals. Team coaching has also been developed and operational management occurs through performance management leaders, who are expected to fulfil their role using a coaching approach.

The line manager as coach

KPMG's coaching culture is now firmly embedded. The organisation employs its own full-time coaches and all its performance management leaders are expected to adopt a coaching style in the way that they interact with their staff. The firm are also exploring new and innovative ways of developing those people whom the business has identified as having particularly strong capability as a coach in addition to their very strong client skills. Coaching conversations are, therefore, part of 'business as normal' at KPMG and a good level of collective trust in the value and credibility of coaching as a style of management has been achieved.

In a service-oriented organisation like KPMG, where time away from client-facing activities is always under pressure, it has been important for managers to appreciate the value of the investment of their time and that of their team members in coaching processes. Although practice and opinion can vary in different functional parts of the business, there has been progress towards a situation where a coaching style of management is seen as a way of being a manager rather than an extra requirement on top of the 'day job'. The crucial factor here has been the attitudes and expectations of executive-level partners.

Where now for coaching?

KPMG has developed its leading position within the professional services market by recruiting, developing and retaining talented individuals. Coaching has become an accepted part of enabling all partners and staff within the organisation to respond flexibly to client and business requirements. This commitment has not changed as economic circumstances have altered, but KPMG has been prepared to take bold and creative action to ensure that they continue to develop and retain high-performing employees during times of business uncertainty.

In January 2009 KPMG recognised the need to respond to potential fluctuations in demand for its services without reverting to staff redundancies. The 'Flexible Futures' package has been put forward to ensure that the organisation is flexible enough to respond proactively and positively to any change in the market while also retaining and developing talented employees. The scheme is designed to allow KPMG to request that employees who agree to the change can be required to work a four-day week or take between four and 12 weeks' sabbatical at 30% of their pay. The proposed change to the terms and conditions will last for 18 months, and the maximum salary loss in one year will be capped at 20%. The firm will continue to provide full benefits throughout that period.

The provision of coaching, like the proactive approach to dealing with challenging business conditions, represents part of a wider employment approach that seeks to value and retain talent and build trust and commitment. KPMG's flexible coaching provision is well placed to succeed in spite of inhospitable economic circumstances. The infrastructure is robust and the model has been seen to be cost-effective. For KPMG coaching is a business issue, an important part of ensuring that partners and staff can continue to develop flexible, creative and customer-focused approaches to the delivery of its high-quality professional services.

IMPLICATIONS FOR MANAGERS AND HR PROFESSIONALS

The model of coaching at the sharp end developed here (see Figure 9 on page 33) provides a framework through which HR professionals and their senior management colleagues can move forward with the development of a coaching style of management. The report has identified a number of important issues with implications for both HR professionals and their line management colleagues.

Line managers are crucial for people management and development, whether their organisations are doing well or struggling to adapt to current economic circumstances. Coaching has become a widely used tool in organisations and those that are able to develop a coaching style of management as part of a more general participative management style can realise benefits such as improved communication processes, higher productivity, greater clarity about goals and objectives, and enhanced staff engagement.

Managers and HR practitioners who are considering whether a coaching culture is appropriate for their organisational circumstances may find that the questions that have been adapted from those used for the Coaching at Work discussion groups offer a useful way to review the issues:

❖ Why bother with coaching? What does a 'coaching culture' have to offer managers and employees in your organisation(s)?

❖ What are the obstacles to coaching in your organisation(s)?

❖ Can a line manager also be a coach? What current organisational factors encourage this and what factors make it difficult or impossible?

❖ Are top managers committed to coaching in the organisation? If yes – why? If no – why?

Additionally, the development of a coaching style of management requires that:

- Coaching is seen by top managers as a business issue rather than a learning and development department initiative.

- Senior managers communicate their commitment to coaching and role-model coaching characteristics in a consistent way.

- Clarity about coaching roles and expectations is achieved and clearly communicated.

- Consistent attention is given to the time and resource constraints facing all managers, particularly those closest to 'the sharp end'.

- Appropriate and relevant training and support is offered to enable managers to develop and maintain coaching characteristics as part of their 'management repertoire'.

- Effective teamworking and relationships between and within teams is fostered and encouraged.

- Managers are encouraged rather than inhibited from developing confidence in their coaching capability.

APPENDIX 1: THE RESEARCH PROJECT

In October 2008 the CIPD appointed members of the University of Portsmouth Business School to undertake the *Coaching at the Sharp End* research project. The research was commissioned to assess the implications of the devolution of coaching to line managers and to provide practical guidance appropriate for line managers to enhance their effectiveness in their role as coach.

PROJECT OBJECTIVES

The specific project objectives were:

❖ to investigate the implications of the development of a coaching culture for the role of line managers

❖ to examine the extent to which line managers report using behaviours associated with a coaching style of management

❖ to assess the individual and organisational influences on a coaching style of management

❖ to develop a framework through which HR professionals can work with line management colleagues to foster 'managers as coaches'.

DATA COLLECTION

Data were gathered from three sources:

❖ discussion groups organised as part of the CIPD Coaching at Work Conference, which took place in November 2008

❖ four semi-structured interviews with an HR or learning and training practitioner with experience of developing the role of the line manager as coach in their organisation; these were held during November and December 2008

❖ responses to an online survey between 17 December 2008 and 21 January 2009 – there were 534 responses by line manager respondents from organisations within the public, private and not-for-profit sectors. Thirteen responses were deemed ineligible as the respondent was not responsible for the direct management of any staff and these were discounted, leaving a response size of 521.

RESEARCH DESIGN

An incremental approach to the research process, which commenced in October 2008, was adopted as follows:

❖ The construction of questions for the discussion groups at the Coaching at Work Conference and the organisational interviews was informed by the literature about coaching at work.

❖ The construction of questions for the survey was informed by the literature about coaching and management and leadership behaviours as well as the issues emerging from the discussion groups and organisational interviews.

SAMPLING APPROACH

A purposive sampling strategy was used for the discussion groups and organisational interviews. Expert respondents formed the basis for these data sources; those who attended the CIPD Coaching at Work Conference were HR or coaching professionals with experience of or interest in the promotion of coaching within the workplace. The discussion groups took place on 25 November 2008 and 95 people from 69 different organisations participated. The organisational interviews were held between 4 November and 22 December 2008. The following organisations participated in the organisational interviews:

❖ VT Group plc

❖ KPMG

❖ Southern Railway

❖ Child Benefit and Tax Credit Office.

Line managers from ten organisations participated in the *Managing at the Sharp End* web-based survey. The participating organisations included:

- Bromley Mytime Leisure Trust
- The Children's Society
- Institute of Leadership and Management
- London Underground – Operations
- Middlesex University
- Ministry of Justice
- Napp Pharmacueticals Ltd
- Red Funnel Group
- VT Group plc.

DISCUSSION GROUP PROTOCOL

A written briefing about the discussion group questions was provided as part of the delegate packs for the CIPD Coaching at Work Conference. Delegates all tackled the same broad questions (see Chapter 2, page 7) and participants generated a written summary of the points that were made.

INTERVIEW PROTOCOL

Interviewees were given the same advance briefing and the same questions were asked in each case (see Chapter 2, page 7). Interviewees were reassured that the purpose of the research was to find out about their perceptions about emerging practice in their organisation. Interviews were all audio-recorded (with permission) and transcribed for later analysis.

SURVEY PROTOCOL

Each participating organisation was provided with a separate hyperlink through which their line managers could access the online survey. Responses from each organisation were stored separately (to enable a data summary to be provided for each organisation) and a merged data set was also generated to enable an analysis of the data set as a whole. Managers were not asked to indicate the organisational sector in which they worked (public, private or not-for-profit) because these were derived from the discrete data sets. A small number of respondents were members of the UK Institute of Leadership and Management, whose employment sector is not known.

DATA ANALYSIS

Interview data were analysed using the NVivo 7 qualitative data analysis software. Recurring themes from the discussion group data and the interview transcripts were identified and these themes were used as a basis for coding and analysis of the data.

Survey data were analysed using the SPSS software. Descriptive frequencies were produced for the data set as a whole and for each of the employment sectors. This identified that the responses represented a normal distribution. The main analytical tools that formed the basis of the subsequent interpretation of the data were:

- principal component analysis (a form of factor analysis)
- Cronbach Alpha reliability test
- Pearsons correlation test.

ETHICS

The research was undertaken in accordance with the ethical guidelines of the University of Portsmouth Business School.

DISSEMINATION

The key conclusions from the research were used to inform the development of the CIPD *Coaching at the Sharp End* online tool, which was published in April 2009.

APPENDIX 2: SURVEY RESPONSES

The frequency of responses to the survey instrument are summarised here.

Section 1 (n = 521) (%)	
Are you (please choose **only one** of the following):	
Male	48.0
Female	52.0
Your age range (please choose **only one** of the following):	
Under 25	1.5
25–34	18.0
35–44	33.4
45–54	33.2
55–64	13.4
Over 64	0.4
How many people report directly to you (please write your answer here)?	
Which best reflects your level in the organisation hierarchy (please choose **only one** of the following)?	
First-line manager	42.0
Middle manager	47.4
Top-level/board manager	10.6
If you have management qualifications, please select the highest level (please choose **only one** of the following):	
None	46.3
NVQ Level 2	4.8
NVQ Level 3	5.2
NVQ Level 4	6.7

Business qualification, for example degree, DMS, CIPD	37.0

How long have you been in your current position (please choose **only one** of the following)?

Less than 3 months	3.1
3 months – 1 year	14.8
1–5 years	51.2
More than 5 years	30.9

Section 2: Think about the people you manage (please choose the appropriate response for each item) (n = 521) (%)

	Applies to all people you manage	Applies to some people you manage	Applies to no people you manage
Their duties are so simple that almost anyone could perform them after some instruction and practice.	8.3	33.2	58.5
Rules and guidelines exist for their tasks, which they have to follow.	62.4	28.2	9.4
They work as a team and I don't have to interfere.	14.8	70.2	15.0
Their competence and knowledge means they solve all their problems on their own.	14.6	77.5	7.9
It is best all round if I just tell them what to do all the time.	1.0	28.8	70.2

Section 3: Think about how you treat the people you manage (in the last 3 months) (please choose only one of the following) (n = 521) (%)

They are alike and I mostly treat them the same.	5.0
They are alike and I mostly treat them differently.	1.3
They are different and I mostly treat them differently.	64.1
They are different and I mostly treat them the same.	29.6

Section 4: Think about your behaviour in the last 3 months with the people you manage (please choose the appropriate response for each item) (n = 521) (%)

	All of the time	Most of the time	Some of the time	None of the time
I have helped them all develop themselves as individuals.	17.1	47.8	33.4	1.7
I am very good at observing their work to guide my management of them.	17.9	53.7	27.3	1.2
I am very good at helping them all to express their own action plans.	15.0	52.0	29.9	3.1
The time I spend helping them is not valued by any of them.	1.9	6.0	33.8	58.0
I ask questions of all of them rather than providing solutions.	9.4	50.9	36.3	3.8
I find it difficult to raise their performance shortfalls directly and promptly with all the people I manage.	1.0	5.6	50.3	43.2

Section 5 (n = 521) (%)

	All of the time	Most of the time	Some of the time	None of the time
I give them all a good share of the decision-making.	17.3	55.9	24.6	2.3
I actively help them all find and get training/ learning to improve their performance and skills.	30.7	45.5	21.9	1.9
I am very conscientious in giving them all feedback on the work – positive and negative.	38.4	48.9	12.3	0.4
Whenever I meet them I spend more time listening than questioning.	19.4	53.2	26.5	1.0
If any of them has a good idea I always use it.	32.1	50.6	16.7	1.0
I want them all to be able to solve problems for themselves.	54.7	39.2	5.8	0.4

Section 6: The last two screens asked you about the following behaviours with your staff: sharing decision-making, making action plans, listening, questioning, giving feedback, developing them personally and professionally. In an ideal world, would you like to have done more or less of this type of work with them? (Please choose only one of the following.) (n = 521) (%)

More	54.5
Less	2.9
Neither, it has been just right	42.6

[Only answer this question if you answered 'More' to the last question] What are the barriers? (Please distribute 100 marks between the various options according to their importance.) (n = 284) (mean)

I haven't the time.	61.99
I don't know where to start.	3.76
They are difficult people.	9.43
I lack the skills.	6.2
It's not my style.	2.49
I haven't got the patience.	1.9
It's not part of my job.	1.82
No reward for me.	1.67
It's not the style in our organisation.	9.68
My staff would leave.	1.05

Section 7: In an ideal world, what would be helpful to improve these activities with the people you manage? (Reminder – the activities are: sharing decision-making, making action plans, listening, questioning, giving feedback, developing them personally and professionally.) Please choose the appropriate response for each item (n = 521) (%)

	Very helpful	Helpful	Not very helpful	Not helpful
In-house training course	29.4	50.1	14.2	6.3
External training course	18.0	52.2	21.3	8.4
Being given space to learn by trial and error	20.0	48.9	22.1	9.0
Advice and guidance from a senior manager/mentor	33.4	54.5	7.7	4.4
One-to-one coaching from my manager	24.8	49.3	17.3	8.6

Section 8: Please select the number which best describes your level of agreement regarding the people you manage (please choose the appropriate response for each item) (n = 521) (%)

	1 = Strongly agree	2	3	4	5	6	7 = Strongly disagree
I admire their professional skills.	18.8	37.9	26.9	9.1	3.8	2.6	0.8
I respect their knowledge and competence on the job.	33.4	39.0	17.1	5.4	3.8	1.0	0.4
I work for them beyond what is specified in my job description.	27.8	35.7	21.3	9.4	2.7	1.7	1.3
I am willing to apply extra effort to further their interests.	34.9	44.0	14.4	4.2	1.3	0.8	0.4
I do not mind working hard for them.	38.4	44.0	10.2	3.3	2.9	0.8	0.6
I am impressed with their knowledge of the job.	27.1	39.0	21.7	6.3	4.4	1.2	0.4

Section 9: Please choose the number which best describes your level of agreement to each statement. Please choose the appropriate response for each item. (n = 521) (%)

	1 = Completely true	2	3	4	5	6 = Not at all true
I can remain calm when facing difficulties in my job because I can rely on my abilities.	30.5	48.6	16.5	3.6	0.8	0
When I am confronted with a problem in my job I can usually find several solutions.	25.1	53.0	18.6	2.3	0.8	0.2
Whatever comes my way in my job I can usually handle it.	32.8	51.2	12.9	2.1	1.0	0
My past experiences in my job have prepared me well for my occupational future.	36.7	42.8	13.4	4.0	1.7	1.3
I meet the goals that I set for myself in my job.	20.9	52.0	20.9	4.4	1.3	0.4
I feel prepared for most of the demands in my job.	23.8	52.2	15.4	6.3	1.7	0.6

APPENDIX 3: DATA ANALYSIS

FREQUENCY DISTRIBUTION

Descriptive frequencies for the sample respondents as a whole are shown in Appendix 2. Responses to most Section 1 questions were normally distributed across the range of responses (except Question 5). Other sections showed a

general skew towards positive responses as would be expected from a self-reporting survey.

The survey structure and a summary of the distribution pattern of responses are as follows:

Section	Theme	Question no.	Range	Mean	Standard deviation
1	Biographical/demographic	1	2	1.48	0.5
		2	6	3.4	0.993
		3	n/a		
		4	3	1.69	0.654
		5	5	1.83	1.851
		6	4	3.1	0.756
2	Work and task environment	1	3	1.5	0.645
		2	3	2.53	0.662
		3	3	2.0	0.546
		4	3	1.93	0.47
		5	3	1.31	0.482
3	Personal approach to management	1	4	3.18	0.69

Section	Theme	Question no.	Range	Mean	Standard deviation
4	Coaching behaviours (1)	1	4	1.8	0.732
		2	4	1.88	0.696
		3	4	1.79	0.727
		4	4	0.61	0.696
		5	4	1.65	0.701
		6	4	2.36	0.632
5	Coaching behaviours (2)	1	4	1.88	0.705
		2	4	2.05	0.775
		3	4	2.25	0.677
		4	4	1.91	0.7
		5	4	2.13	0.713
		6	4	2.48	0.623
6	Personal management approach	1	3	2.52	0.555
7	Support and development	1	4	3.02	0.831
		2	4	2.8	0.832
		3	4	2.8	0.861
		4	4	3.17	0.748
		5	4	2.9	0.87
8	Manager–team relationship	1	7	2.52	1.233
		2	7	2.12	1.142
		3	7	2.34	1.269
		4	7	1.97	1.001
		5	7	1.93	1.067
		6	7	2.27	1.161
9	Manager self-confidence	1	6	1.96	0.827
		2	6	2.01	0.794
		3	6	1.87	0.782
		4	6	1.95	1.016
		5	6	2.14	0.871
		6	6	2.12	0.938

FACTOR ANALYSIS (PRINCIPAL COMPONENT ANALYSIS)

Some groups of questions in the survey set out to examine variables that are multidimensional in nature:

❖ coaching characteristics

❖ manager self-confidence

❖ work and task environment

❖ manager–team relationships.

A number of different questions were included within the groups for these variables and it was intended that these questions would cluster together to collectively represent these broader variables. The principal component test was used to assess the extent to which different questions could be considered as a coherent 'cluster'. The principal component test creates a matrix of correlations and assesses the variance that is accounted for by each of the questions in the clusters. Results (factor loadings) of 0.4 or above were taken as valid.

A Cronbach Alpha test of reliability was applied to each of the clusters isolated in this way. A Cronbach Alpha (α) of 0.75 indicates a good level of reliability.

Factor analysis results are indicated in Tables 10–12. The factor analysis for manager self-confidence identified that the group of questions are so robust that only one component could be extracted (and therefore the cluster was confirmed). The Cronbach Alpha reliability (α) for the six questions taken together was 0.85.

Table 10: Coaching characteristics factor analysis*

	Primary coaching α= .78	Mature coaching α= .48
I have helped them all develop themselves as individuals.	.690	
I am very good at observing their work to guide my management of them.	.762	
I am very good at helping them all to express their own action plans.	.739	
I ask questions of them all rather than providing solutions.		.440
I give them all a good share of the decision-making.		.422
I actively help them all find and get training/learning to improve their performance and skills.	.649	
I am very conscientious in giving them all feedback on the work – positive and negative.	.668	
If any of them has a good idea, I always use it.		.604
I want them all to be able to solve problems for themselves.		.782

* Extraction method = principal component analysis

Table 11: Work and task environment factor analysis*

	Standard work α= .45	Autonomy α= .55
Their duties are so simple that almost anyone could perform them after some instruction and practice.	.738	
Rules and guidelines exist for their tasks, which they have to follow.	.659	
They work as a team and I don't have to interfere.		.838
Their competence and knowledge means they solve all their problems on their own.		.807
It is best all round if I just tell them what to do all the time.	.681	

* Extraction method = principal component analysis

Table 12: Manager–team relationship factor analysis*

	(αfor all 6 factors = .86)	
	Respect	Effort
I admire their professional skills.	.889	
I respect their knowledge and competence on the job.	.884	
I work for them beyond what is specified in my job description.		.820
I am willing to apply extra effort to further their interests.		.879
I do not mind working hard for them.		.841
I am impressed with their knowledge of the job.	.868	

* Extraction method = principal component analysis

TESTS OF CORRELATION

The Pearson correlation test was used to examine the strength of association between variables included in the survey. In addition to an examination of association between demographic variables (such as age, gender, experience in current post, and so on) and the perceived usefulness of different training support methods, the Pearson test was used to assess the correlation between the following broader variables:

- ❖ primary coaching characteristics
- ❖ mature coaching characteristics
- ❖ work and task environment
    - ❖ autonomy
    - ❖ standardised work
- ❖ manager self-confidence
- ❖ manager–team relationship.

Tables 13–15 show the correlation tables. With a sample size of over 500, a correlation 'rating' of 0.1–0.4 can be regarded as a good level of association. A correlation of more than 0.4 represents a strong level of association between the two variables.

Table 13: Correlations between coaching characteristics and other variables

		Primary coaching	Mature coaching
Gender	Pearson Correlation	.112	.038
	Sig. (2-tailed)	.010	.383
Age	Pearson Correlation	-.020	.082
	Sig. (2-tailed)	.645	.063
Seniority	Pearson Correlation	.068	.231(**)
	Sig. (2-tailed)	.123	.000
Qualifications	Pearson Correlation	.077	.130(**)
	Sig. (2-tailed)	.077	.003
Tenure in this position	Pearson Correlation	.121(**)	.067
	Sig. (2-tailed)	.006	.127
Autonomy	Pearson Correlation	.087	.144(**)
	Sig. (2-tailed)	.046	.001
Standardised work	Pearson Correlation	.011	.131(**)
	Sig. (2-tailed)	.802	.003
Manager–team relationship	Pearson Correlation	.371(**)	.307(**)
	Sig. (2-tailed)	.000	.000
Manager self-confidence	Pearson Correlation	.435(**)	.203(**)
	Sig. (2-tailed)	.000	.000
Primary coaching	Pearson Correlation	1	.418(**)
	Sig. (2-tailed)		.000
Mature coaching	Pearson Correlation	.418(**)	1
	Sig. (2-tailed)	.000	

** Correlation is significant at the 0.01 level (2-tailed).

Table 14: Correlations between training and support and other variables

		In-house course	External course	Trial and error	Advice/ guidance	One-to-one
In-house course	Pearson		.517(**)	.176(**)	.290(**)	.304(**)
	Sig. (2-tailed)		.000	.000	.000	.000
External course	Pearson	.517(**)		.126(**)	.262(**)	.222(**)
	Sig. (2-tailed)	.000		.004	.000	.000
Trial and error	Pearson	.176(**)	.126(**)		.214(**)	.148(**)
	Sig. (2-tailed)	.000	.004		.000	.001
Advice/guidance	Pearson	.290(**)	.262(**)	.214(**)		.622(**)
	Sig. (2-tailed)	.000	.000	.000		.000
One-to-one	Pearson	.304(**)	.222(**)	.148(**)	.622(**)	
	Sig. (2-tailed)	.000	.000	.001	.000	
Gender	Pearson	-.052	-.017	.073	.055	-.020
	Sig. (2-tailed)	.236	.703	.095	.207	.649
Age	Pearson	-.005	-.058	-.101	-.169(**)	-.130(**)
	Sig. (2-tailed)	.906	.187	.021	.000	.003
Seniority	Pearson	-.138(**)	.010	.024	.007	-.051
	Sig. (2-tailed)	.002	.812	.589	.879	.247
Qualifications	Pearson	.001	.088	.098	-.003	.009
	Sig. (2-tailed)	.974	.044	.025	.938	.837
Tenure in this position	Pearson	.054	-.075	-.010	-.088	-.064
	Sig. (2-tailed)	.216	.087	.813	.045	.144

** Correlation is significant at the 0.01 level (2-tailed).

Table 15: Correlations between training and support and coaching characteristics

		Primary coaching	Mature coaching
In-house course	Pearson Correlation	.245(**)	
	Sig. (2-tailed)	.000	
External course	Pearson Correlation	.188(**)	
	Sig. (2-tailed)	.000	.
Trial and error	Pearson Correlation	.142(**)	.183(**)
	Sig. (2-tailed)	.001	.000
Advice/guidance	Pearson Correlation	.154(**)	
	Sig. (2-tailed)	.000	
One-to-one	Pearson Correlation	.111	
	Sig. (2-tailed)	.011	

** Correlation is significant at the 0.01 level (2-tailed).

APPENDIX 4: BEHAVIOURS, ATTRIBUTES, STYLES RELATING TO COACHING IDENTIFIED IN PUBLISHED QUESTIONNAIRES AND INVENTORIES

Ellinger et al (2003)	✧ Effective development dialogue ✧ Seek and provide constructive feedback ✧ Provide appropriate resources for performance ✧ Effective questioning ✧ Set appropriate expectations
Griffiths and Campbell (2008)	✧ Establish trust ✧ Active listening ✧ Powerful questioning ✧ Direct communication ✧ Suggest (development) opportunities ✧ Plan and set goals ✧ Manage progress and accountability
Hawkins and Smith (2006)	✧ Contracting/negotiating skills ✧ Listening skills ✧ Questioning skills ✧ Explore development needs ✧ Planning ✧ Giving and receiving feedback

De Haan and Burger (2005)	❖ Relationship skills/management of expectations
	❖ Behavioural styles:
	  ❖ discovering
	  ❖ releasing
	  ❖ challenging
	  ❖ prescribing
	  ❖ informing
	  ❖ supporting

Grant (2007)	❖ Establishing appropriate goals ❖ Establish effective rapport/relationship ❖ Managing processes ❖ Understanding and using emotions
Clutterbuck and Lane (2004)*	❖ Development orientation ❖ Communication skills ❖ Self-awareness ❖ Mutual support and development ❖ Goal-focused ❖ Relationship skills ❖ Listening skills
Ellis (2004)	❖ Effective development dialogue ❖ Seek and provide constructive feedback ❖ Listening skills ❖ Questioning skills ❖ Explore development needs ❖ Relationship skills ❖ Plan and set goals ❖ Manage progress and accountability

* This research focused on the skills and behaviours of mentors rather than coaches.

REFERENCES

ALEXANDER, G. and RENSHAW, B. (2005) *Supercoaching: the missing ingredient for high performance*. London: Random House.

BLESSINGWHITE. (2008) *The coaching conundrum 2009: building a coaching culture that drives organizational success*. Skillman, NJ: BlessingWhite.

CHARTERED INSTITUTE OF PERSONNEL AND DEVELOPMENT. (2004) *Helping people learn: strategies for moving from training to learning*. London: CIPD.

CHARTERED INSTITUTE OF PERSONNEL AND DEVELOPMENT. (2005) *Training to learning [online]*. Change Agenda. London: CIPD. Available at: http://www.cipd.co.uk/subjects/lrnanddev/general/train2lrn0405.htm

CHARTERED INSTITUE OF PERSONNEL AND DEVELOPMENT. (2008a) *Coaching and buying coaching services*. Guide. London: CIPD.

CHARTERED INSTITUTE OF PERSONNEL AND DEVELOPMENT. (2008b) *Learning and development [online]*. Annual survey report. London: CIPD. Available at: http://www.cipd.co.uk/subjects/lrnanddev/general/_lrngdevsvy.htm

CHARTERED INSTITUTE OF PERSONNEL AND DEVELOPMENT. (2008c) *Learning and the line: assessing and enhancing the role and contribution of line managers in learning, training and development [online]*. Practical tool. Available at: http://www.cipd.co.uk/NR/rdonlyres/D34E7BC5-2CE5-4CC8-87DD-3F7141C2D477/0/learningandtheline.pdf.

CHARTERED INSTITUTE OF PERSONNEL AND DEVELOPMENT. (2008d) *Who learns at work? Employees' experiences of workplace learning [online]*. Research Insight. London: CIPD. Available at: http://www.cipd.co.uk/subjects/lrnanddev/general/_wholrnswrk.htm.

CLUTTERBUCK, D. and LANE, G. (2004) *The situational mentor: an international review of competencies and capabilities in mentoring*. Aldershot: Gower.

CLUTTERBUCK, D. and MEGGINSON, D. (2005) *Making coaching work: creating a coaching culture*. London: CIPD.

D'ABATE, P., EDDY, E.R and TANNENBAUM, S.I. (2003) What's in a name? A literature-based approach to understanding mentoring, coaching and other constructs that describe developmental interactions. *Human Resource Development Review*. Vol 2, No 4. pp360–384.

DE HAAN, E. and BURGER, Y. (2005) *Coaching with colleagues: an action guide for one-to-one learning*. Basingstoke: Palgrave Macmillan.

ELLINGER, A.D. (2005) Contextual factors influencing learning in a workplace setting: the case of 'reinventing itself company'. *Human Resource Development Quarterly*. Vol 16, No 3. pp389–415.

ELLINGER, A.D., ELLINGER, A.E. et al (2003) Supervisory coaching behavior, employee satisfaction, and warehouse employee performance: a dyadic perspective in the distribution industry. *Human Resource Development Quarterly*. Vol 14, No 4. pp435–457.

ELLIS, C.W. (2004) *Management skills for new managers*. New York: Amacom.

GRANT, A.M. (2007) Enhancing coaching skills and emotional intelligence through training. *Industrial and Commercial Training*. Vol 39, No 5. pp257–266.

GRIFFITHS, K. and CAMPBELL, M. (2008) Regulating the regulators: paving the way for international, evidence-based coaching standards. *International Journal of Evidence Based Coaching and Mentoring*. Vol 6, No 1. pp19–31.

HAWKINS, P. and SMITH, N. (2006) *Coaching, mentoring and organizational consultancy: supervision and development*. Maidenhead: Open University Press.

HOLBECHE, L. (2005) *The high performance organization: creating dynamic stability and sustainable success*. London: Butterworth-Heinemann.

HOWE, M. (2008) Coaching at the crossroads – is it enough to position coaching activities with line managers? In: *Coaching and buying coaching services*. Guide. London: CIPD. pp52–54.

HUTCHINSON, S. and PURCELL, J. (2003) *Bringing policies to life: the vital role of front line managers*. London: CIPD.

HUTCHINSON, S. and PURCELL, J. (2007) *Line managers in reward, learning and development*. Research into Practice Report. London: CIPD.

IVES, Y. (2008) What is coaching? An exploration of conflicting paradigms. *International Journal of Evidence Based Coaching and Mentoring*. Vol 6, No 2. pp100–113.

JACKSON, P. (2005) How do we describe coaching? An exploratory development of a typology of coaching based on the accounts of UK-based practitioners. *International Journal of Evidence Based Coaching and Mentoring*. Vol 3, No 2. pp45–60.

JARVIS, J. (2004) *Coaching and buying coaching services*. London: CIPD.

JERMIER, J.M. and KERR, S. (1997) Substitutes for leadership: their meaning and measurement – contextual recollections and current observations. *Leadership Quarterly*. Vol 8, No 2. pp95–103.

KERR, S. and JERMIER, J.M. (1978) Substitutes for leadership: their meaning and measurement. *Organizational Behavior and Human Performance*. Vol 22. pp375–403.

KNIGHTS, A. and POPPLETON, A. (2008) *Developing coaching capability in organisations*. London: CIPD.

MAYO, A. (2008) Opinion: everyone wants to be a coach. *Training Zone*. 11 February. Available at: http://www.trainingzone.co.uk/cgi-bin/item.cgi?id=179243 [Accessed 16 February 2009].

MEGGINSON, D. and CLUTTERBUCK, D. (2006) Creating a coaching culture. *Industrial and Commercial Training*. Vol 38, No 5. pp232–237.

PARSLOE, E. and WRAY, M. (2000) *Coaching and mentoring*. London: Kogan Page.

PODSAKOFF, P.M. and MACKENZIE, S.B. (1997) Kerr and Jermier's subsitutes for leadership model: background, empirical assessment, and suggestions for future research. *Leadership Quarterly*. Vol 8, No 2. pp117–125.

PURCELL, J. and HUTCHINSON, S. (2007) Front-line managers as agents in the HRM–performance causal chain: theory, analysis and evidence. *Human Resource Management Journal*. Vol 17, No 1. pp3–20.

RIGOTTI, T., SCHYNS, B. and MOHR, G. (2008) A short version of the occupational self-efficacy scale: structural and construct validity across five countries. *Journal of Career Assessment*. Vol 16, No 2. pp238–255.

ROCK, D. and DONDE, R. (2008) Driving organisational change with internal coaching programmes: part 2. *Industrial and Commercial Training*. Vol 40, No 2. pp75–80.

THOMAS, A.M. (1995) *Coaching for staff development*. Leicester: BPS Books.

WHITMORE, J. (2002) *Coaching for performance: growing people, performance and purpose*. London: Nicholas Brealey.